JESUS CAN...
HEAL YOUR HURTS

Christian Writers Collective, LLC
Stephanie K. Reynolds, Founder

ISBN 979-8-9862076-2-9 (paperback)
ISBN 979-8-9862076-3-6 (e-book)

Jesus Can . . . Heal Your Hurts is dedicated

to Jesus and to every writer in this book,

especially to those who are also

in the first book of this series,

Jesus Can . . . Give You A New Life.

May the Lord richly bless you for joining

the CWC when it required faith to do so.

May He add at least thirty more writers,

just like you, to Book 3,

Jesus Can . . . Give You Purpose,

coming soon.

Table of Contents

Introduction

With the release of this book, *Jesus Can* is now officially a series. I express my joy for this fact with a simple smile on the outside, but inside I'm privately jumping up and down and shouting, "Hallelujah!" in praise to our Lord. This heartfelt response also serves as a reminder to review all that God has done to make this day a reality.

Perhaps the only thing more exciting than reviewing this reminder is looking forward to the impact that these books will have on the mission of expanding God's kingdom now that He has clearly and personally demonstrated that He "is able to do immeasurably more than all we ask or imagine" (Ephesians 3:20a).

Below are just a few of the things that I imagined that God would provide a way for me to accomplish when He called me to publish "the Christian version of *Chicken Soup for the Soul®*" (CSS):

- Feature 100 Christian writers in every book
- Publish 10-12 different titles in the *Jesus Can* book series every year
- Sell as many or more books per month than the 1.6 million books that CSS has been averaging since 1994

I'll stop writing now so that you can go ahead and start

reading this book. I'm so grateful for the thirty writers featured in this book. I'm especially grateful for the fact that fifteen of them were part of our inaugural group of thirty writers in Book 1 of our series, *Jesus Can...Give You A New Life!* This book is dedicated to Jesus and the forty-five writers in both books.

Please pause after you read this and pray for the request that you'll find below. I thank you for your prayers and for supporting our mission to spread the gospel far and wide by buying this book. May the Lord richly bless you, more than you can ask or imagine. Amen.

—Stephanie

P.S. Please join me in praying that the very first Christian writer that I ever wrote to request their testimony for Book 1 of this series would be featured in Book 3 of this series, *Jesus Can...Give You Purpose.* That writer's name is Dr. Tony Evans. Feel free to drop him a letter or an email if you'd like to take the additional step of putting your prayer in writing.

You can visit this page of the tonyevans.org website for contact information: https://tonyevans.org/contact

Again, I thank you so much for your prayers and practical help. –S.

1

♡ *When I Was Nine Years Old*

▼

by Stephanie Reynolds Founder of the Christian Writers Collective, LLC

I was molested when I was nine years old. What started out as a fun opportunity to spend the night at a friend's house during my fifth summer break from school, ended my care-free joy of childhood. This dramatic change happened just as abruptly as my opening sentence may have taken you from merely reading a book to recalling either being a victim or knowing a victim of this all-too-common-but-seldom-talked-about evil.

At nine years old, I didn't even know that "molested" was the name given to what had happened to me. I learned this word after I told my parents what had happened to me. They called the police, and the police officers called this evil by name. What I did know for certain was that my life would be forever changed after a friend's father isolated me from the other girls at a slumber party and then touched me inappropriately.

I went from the fun-loving life of a nine-year-old child to a life filled with a multitude of fears. I was afraid to be alone, I was afraid to be with strangers, and I was especially afraid of being touched by males of all ages, except babies, toddlers, and my dad. For many years, just a friendly hug brought flashbacks of being a victim. Because of my fears, I learned to exercise great finesse in the art of not being touched. It was a skill that brought with it an inescapable sense of isolation and loneliness. The pain of my new "skill" was almost as intense as the hurt that led me to cultivate it. Even as a child, I knew this was no way to live. I wanted to get over being afraid and stop jumping every time a man brushed up against me. I wanted to be healed.

Shortly after the incident, I started spontaneously breaking into tears while lying in bed at night, alone in the darkness. This was the time and place where my memories hurt the most. Ironically, this was also the place where I felt as if I were healing too. For the next twelve years, my pain seemed to decrease as my healing increased, while I was lying in bed at night, alone in the dark.

One night, when I was twenty-one years old, just as quickly as I had broken into tears countless times for a dozen years, I decided that I would stop crying. I was determined to make that night the last time I'd ever cry about the evil that had happened to me when I was nine years old. From that night on, I considered myself healed.

There was just one problem with the "healing" that I experienced when I was twenty-one years old: it was only a self-healing. In my case, this self-healing required continuous self-deception in order to remain effective beyond the 1.5 seconds it takes to say, "I am healed," regardless of whether you say it out loud or in your head. I was a lot like alcoholics and drug addicts that keep telling themselves—and everyone within earshot—"I can quit anytime! I just don't want to quit." This is a lie, and everyone who hears it knows that it's a lie…except for the person telling it. Mental health professionals call this denial. The Bible calls it sin. No matter what you call it, it's a miserable way to live.

At twenty-one years old, I was so proud of myself for having the courage to graduate from having a fear of being touched by men to enjoying being sexually intimate with them. Considering I'd only slept with two men—a young man in the military that I dated for 2½ years, followed by the boyfriend that I rebelliously eloped with after dating about that same amount of time—the world would have considered me "slow." Compared to what the media was reporting about college students in the '80s, I was slow! But by God's standards, I had slept with two men too many outside of the commitment and safety of marriage.

Eloping against my parents' wishes and without their knowledge was *my* plan, not His. While God has forgiven me of these sins and many, many more, He has left their natural consequences in place. It's not His fault that I kept choosing to believe easy lies over the hard truth that my life was a miserable mess, especially when it was compared to the purpose-filled life that He had planned for me.

Less than one hour after eloping, I became acutely aware of the fact that the level of denial that I usually practiced wasn't going to be sufficient to cover the mistake I had just made. I can't remember if my new husband carried me over the threshold. Yet, forty years later, I can still see him bursting through the door of our first foolish financial decision—an overpriced one bedroom apartment at a luxury complex—and working himself into a fit. Why? Because our approximately fifteen-year-old car, without a single blemish on the body, had stalled on the way home from the courthouse. His tears and temper kept escalating until I agreed to cosign for a loan to buy a brand new car with a price tag that was equivalent to over half of my pay for my first full-time, post-college job in my chosen profession. Mental health professionals call this gaslighting—a very simple, but effective manipulation technique. I call it God allowing me to deal with the consequences of my sinful choices. He knew, long before time began, exactly how long it was going to take me to grow sick and tired of living a life of lies—of my own creation or someone else's.

This is where the retelling of the story of how God healed me becomes challenging to write and even more challenging to understand, so I'll just tell you what happened… About six months into our "marriage," my future ex-husband abruptly took a break from gaslighting me, to return to the routine his family maintained while he was growing up. As a child, his family went to church twice on Sunday, plus two to four other days of the week. His personality changed just as abruptly and dramatically as how he was spending his time! Instead of behaving like a bully and gaslighting me, he quietly, humbly, and frequently invited me to go to church with him. It was easy to say no to this guy, so I did—for about two months.

When I finally said yes to his invitation to join him for church, it was only because his calmer behavior helped me to come out of denial enough to tell myself the truth: all of these sudden changes, combined with all the time that he was spending away from home, suggested that he was having an affair. My only reason for going to church with him that first time was to catch a glimpse of "the other woman."

I didn't see the other woman that first Sunday in church with my husband. That first Sunday was the last Sunday of March 1983, and I was starting my fourth month of pregnancy. What I saw was the genuine kindness of the people who shook my hand and introduced themselves to me. They also mentioned that they had been praying for me to come to church and shared their authentic enthusiasm that God had answered their prayers. This, combined with the message of Jesus's love for me that I heard in every song and that first sermon, made me want to come back whether my husband invited me or not.

God's timing in all this could not have been more perfect. When I came out of denial enough to see the truth that I was deeply in debt because I had allowed myself to be gaslighted by an unfaithful man, receiving Jesus as my Savior was not the first solution I contemplated—suicide was. I visualized in vivid color and detail how I'd end my life and my pain while destroying the brand new car that I cosigned for and that my husband loved so much more than me. I had planned to drive it into a tree or some other immovable object at a destructively high speed. If I had not been pregnant, I probably would have fulfilled this vision. Thankfully, even in my pain, I understood that taking my life would kill my unborn child too. It just didn't seem fair that the only innocent person in our family of three would have to pay for our sins with his life.

It was on my third visit to church with my husband that Jesus gave me a new life! It was Sunday, April 10, 1983. It seemed as if I was the only person the pastor was preaching to that day. By the time he came to the invitation, I had already cried a river of noisy, ugly, but soul-cleansing tears. I ran up front to receive God's free gift of salvation in Jesus as quickly as my pregnancy-swollen feet and ankles would take me!

I now tell people how grateful I am that I was so ignorant on Sunday, April 10, 1983, the day that Jesus gave me a new life! I didn't have any religious habits or false beliefs to confuse me nor hold me back when it was time to make the decision to receive God's gift. It was like learning to play the piano or to touch type for the very first time. It's so much easier to learn to do it right from the beginning than to have to un-learn a lot of bad habits.

April 10, 1983 was the first day that I had ever heard and be-lieved the fact that Jesus is God. This fact, this truth, was life-changing. It changed everything for me that day. I no longer had to live in denial and self-deception. My childhood hurt of being molested was healed the day I received Jesus as my Savior, in part because it was almost trivial compared to the hurt I had inflicted upon myself and my child by mar-rying the man of my choosing, not God's.

Sadly, the season of both my husband and me walking with the Lord and loving each other was short-lived. As is usually the case, the other woman was at work, not at church. We stopped going to church together, and his attempts to gaslight me returned. Being able to see and accept the truth was a mixed blessing. However, it was far better than living a lie every day by choosing to remain in denial.

By the time our son was eleven months old, my future ex-husband had chosen to move out and to take the new car with him. I decided that it was time to stop worrying about what other people might think or say and to end the lie that my marriage had become by obediently filing for a divorce.

April 10, 2022 was my thirty-ninth spiritual birthday and the thirty-ninth anniversary of Jesus beginning the process of genuinely healing the hurt of my being molested when I was nine years old.

What a blessing it would be to know that He used my story to help someone else receive His gift of eternal life in heaven and/or His gift of starting the journey toward genuine healing from being molested as a child or some other form of sexual assault/abuse. I'd count it a privilege to read your story and pray, that in writing your story, God would help you to heal. Feel free to share your story with me by using the CONTACT US form on our website, www.ChristianWritersCollective.com.

I promise to read your story and to pray for you. Unfortunately, as the live-in caregiver for my eighty-nine-year-old dad and the founder of the CWC, I cannot promise that I'll be able to reply to every email that I receive. If you need to have a live phone or text conversation about how Jesus can help heal your hurts, please reach out to NeedHim.org. They have caring volunteers available 24/7.

I'll close by praying that every reader has or will begin to seek the full measure of healing that God has for you. I'm rejoicing in the fact that He is able to heal all of our hurts. Amen.

Stephanie Reynolds, CWC Founder

2

♡ *Songs of the Soul*

▼

by Kitty Foth-Regner

I've been blessed with a largely trouble-free life, suffering only a handful of crushing blows over almost seven decades of living in this fallen world. But those blows were doozies, each one involving the loss of someone I loved dearly. In each case, it was my relationship with the Lord Jesus Christ—or lack of a relationship with Him—that determined how thoroughly, and how quickly, I healed from the pain of these heartaches.

Jesus Can…

"Alone Again, Naturally"

The first loss was my beloved daddy. He dropped dead at age fifty-nine, when I was just seventeen and my mother was fifty-six.

My mother's faith in Jesus Christ was of unfathomable comfort to her in the aftermath of his death, but it did nothing for me. In fact, one thing soon became abundantly clear to me: This loving God I'd been raised on couldn't possibly exist. Within days of the funeral, I'd become a proud and angry atheist.

My new and improved God-free world brought about seismic changes in my thinking. It removed all constraints from my life and opened my heart to every foolish pursuit that crossed my path. That meant a stint in the leftist political extremism of the '70s, followed by a love affair with Betty Friedan's brand of radical feminism—an anti-family and anti-life philosophy that would stick with me for the next three decades.

Still, the pain remained. I tried to kill it with drugs and alcohol. When that didn't work, I dumped the drugs and dove into various worldly obsessions—a blossoming copywriting career, repeated attempts to write the great American novel, and the purchase of and hysterical devotion to an American Saddlebred show horse.

But these were mere distractions. Years after my father's death, I was still sitting alone in my East Side Milwaukee apartment, trying to weep the sorrow out of my system once and for all. Gilbert O'Sullivan's 1974 hit "Alone Again (Naturally)" became my official theme song. It was an anthem to self-pity, and I embraced it wholeheartedly.

"You and Me Against the World"

My father had been dead for thirty years before I experienced another such loss. This time, it was my mother—my beautiful, brave, loving mother whose only flaw was her stubborn belief in this imaginary heavenly Friend of hers.

By this time, I was freshly married to my boyfriend of eighteen years, living in a ranch house near Milwaukee with him and a bevy of dogs and cats, obsessed with ban-the-budget gardening and golf and my now-successful freelance copywriting business.

My mother was living in a nearby nursing home, not in great shape physically but still in full possession of her mental marbles, when we learned that she had inoperable colorectal cancer. The doctors said that she had maybe a couple years to live, but it was less than two weeks later that I got the middle-of-the-night phone call saying that she was gone.

I was devastated. Heartsick. Utterly lost and inconsolable. Singer Helen Reddy's 1974 hit "You and Me Against the World" became the song of my heart.

But this time, I was so broken that I had do something about it: If my mom had been right about this imaginary Friend of hers, if she indeed still existed somewhere out there, I had to find out where and figure out how to get there myself.

And so it was that I plunged headlong into the pursuit of ultimate truth. I started with religious friends of various faiths, but they were no help. They answered my desperate questions about why they believed with a shrug and an "I just believe."

Fortunately, pertinent books started falling into my lap. And so I read, and read some more, focusing on subjects from science to history to prophecy. My first question—is there a God?—was soon answered in the affirmative. The next one was tougher: which God is the real deal?

First, I searched for truth in "cool" belief systems like Hinduism, Buddhism, Islam, and the New Age. But finding nothing even remotely resembling objective truth in any of these religions, I finally turned to my folks' old-fashioned Christianity and the Bible—and found that truth had been there all along, in the person of Jesus Christ, just waiting for me to seek Him. Truth, and the promise of a heavenly forever.

It had taken me fifteen months to get there, but at last I'd found healing for my heartbreak.

"Beyond the Sunset"

Since then, I've had several other world-changing deaths to deal with. But here's the thing: Two decades ago, Jesus Christ healed my hurt once and for all. And because He paid for our sins on the cross, I know this: Those who died in Christ have simply gone on ahead. And one happy day I will see them all again, along with dozens of other dear friends who received Jesus as their Savior while they walked this earth.

The Bible tells us that, if we are His, even the worst hurts of this world occur for our eternal good. As Romans 8:28 proclaims, "…all things work *together* for good to those who love God, to those who are the called according to His purpose" (emphasis added).

I believe this with all my heart, having watched Him use pain to transform my life, my outlook, and my wildest dreams. He even used my hurt to put new songs in my heart, hymns of hope and joy and everlasting peace. Now, instead of weeping,

I rejoice because, as musicians Virgil and Blanche Brock wrote back in 1936, "In that fair homeland, we'll know no parting, beyond the sunset forever more!"

"Happily ever after" is no fairy tale for those who belong to Jesus Christ. He healed my hurt, and He can heal yours too. Why not invite Him to do so today?

Kitty Foth-Regner

Kitty Foth-Regner spent her forty-year copywriting career specializing in scientific subjects. So, it is no surprise that it was the Bible's scientific truth that led her to Christ—a journey she recounted in her memoir *Heaven Without Her*. A long-term-care volunteer since 2000, she's also published *The Song of Sadie Sparrow*, a novel exploring the relationships of three women whose paths cross in an idyllic nursing home.

Visit her at www.EverlastingPlace.com.

3

† *God Honors His Word*

▼

by Tonya Brill

I grew up in the foothills of the Appalachian Mountains. I guess you could say that I came from hillbillies, though none of them looked like "The Beverly Hillbillies" nor acted like them. I came from a dysfunctional family like many people these days. We were poor, and my parents always argued about money and bills. Mom and Dad's saying was, "Money don't grow on trees." I would smile up at Daddy and say, "Yeah, but I wish it did. I would pick you a big bushel full of it."

As I grew into a teenager, life became difficult. Mom was never happy and yelled a lot. Dad hid in the basement. I was molested by one of my brothers. Mom didn't believe me. I didn't tell Dad because Mom said she told Dad everything. I felt unloved and thought nobody cared. So, at age seventeen, I took a handful of speed on a dare because I didn't love me either. I had never done any drugs before. I didn't care if I lived or died. I figured with a handful of speed that my heart would race so fast that maybe it would explode or stop. Like I said, I didn't care.

I wound up in the hospital after scaring everyone including Mom. Only the two people who had been with me when I took the speed knew what I had done. They weren't talking about it. The doctor diagnosed me with gastroenteritis and dehydration. According to the doctor there were several of us in the hospital with the same diagnosis. All I thought was, "Wow, I wasn't the only one to try suicide." God loved me so much that He protected me from death and damage.

It would be a year later that God's plan for my life would begin to reveal itself. Mom started going to church and nagged at me to go. In all honesty, I just went to shut her up. I believed in Jesus as a child but quit believing after what I went through at home. Mom had taken us to different churches before as little kids. I remember some of those "good Christian" people were not very nice. What little five-year-old child wants to hear that they had done something so bad that a man was beaten up and nailed to a cross for it? At five years old I couldn't think of anything that I had done that was so bad that a crowd of people had to murder someone because of me. Talk about a complex. As if home-life wasn't bad enough growing up, I had that heaped on me from some of the churches Mom took us to for their services.

The pastor of this new church was different. There was just something about him that held my eighteen-year-old attention. He spoke of God's Son, Jesus, loving me so much that He would honor His Word. That pastor said to test God's Word to see if He was real and true. I had been without work and needed a job. So I said to God, "You said to ask and I will receive in Jesus' name. I haven't been able to find a job for two months. So, please, give me a job, in Jesus' name." The next day I turned in one more application and was hired immediately. I went through this process two more times with things that I needed. After the third time of God answering my prayers, I said to Him, "You *are* real. I'm yours. I'm sold. Jesus, forgive me and come into my life."

Life has never been the same. I have peace. When I don't, I take it to Jesus. I have joy and can now feel love. God has taken me on a healing journey over many years. I forgave Mom. Her wedding ring should have gone to the oldest daughter. She chose to give it to me, the middle child, long before she ever passed on. I forgave my brother too. God told me that He would remove the pain of molestation as far from me as the east is from the west. Now when I talk about it, it is like it happened to somebody else.

Jesus wants to heal you too. I am in agreement with you that it happens.

Tonya M. Brill

Tonya M. Brill is a writer and photographer residing in the foothills of the Appalachian Mountains. She enjoys nature, her dogs, and spending time with Jesus.

Her website: www.timemadebeautiful.com

4

♡ *Add Something Extra Too*

by Nyla Kay Wilkerson

Holidays are a time for family, friends, food, and fun. They are filled with joy and laughter. Most people are excited about each and every holiday, but there are some that are not.

That actually was me for years. I was angry, bitter, and hurt. When I was just twelve years old my father died. Not only did he die, but he died at home in front of me. Daddy was feeling ill at work and was driven home early. After he had settled in on the living room couch, he had a fatal massive heart attack. It was so traumatic that the event continues to haunt me in nightmares even now.

For years I did not want to go to church on Father's Day after Daddy died. Easter, Thanksgiving, and Christmas were empty without him. I have gotten through that horrible experience, but I will never get over it. It left scars.

I began to pray for peace. Since I had no father, surely Jesus would hear my prayer and fill my emptiness. After a few years, He did. A decade or so after Daddy died, a blessing was given to my mother, younger sister, and me. My Heavenly Father sent a great man who was perfect for our family. I called him Dad. He did not replace my birth father, but he did fill a big void in my life. All girls, no matter what age, need a father. I especially did. Uncles stepped up to help, but it was never the same. Dad was so perfect for us that I was finally able to celebrate Father's Day with happiness and not sorrow. I was able to return to church and celebrate fathers with the other families.

For forty years this remarkable, selfless man was the leader of our family. He and my mother were inseparable and the quintessential Christian married couple. Sadly for us, Dad was called home to heaven in September 2020, but the treasured memories will forever live on in our hearts and minds. Now I rejoice that Dad is at peace and pain-free. I am so thankful that God shared him with us. We rest in the assurance of one day being reunited in heaven for eternity.

Dad was a devoted, loving husband to Mom and the most wonderful father that my sister and I could ever have received. On top of that, he was a grandfather beyond compare to our children. Just ask anyone who called him Pappaw.

Dad was a good example for all fathers. His faith in Jesus was essential in every part of his life. Whenever I needed prayer or had a question about scripture, Dad was the first one I sought. He taught Sunday School and Bible Study, so he knew the Bible inside out. Dad was a giant in faith.

Generosity was one of his gifts. I often watched him anonymously pay for a young family's meal and ask the waitress to add something extra too, like ice cream for dessert. Dad not only gave, but he gave above and beyond. That is how I see God give blessings. He graciously gives not just the minimum but adds even more on too.

Romans 8:28 teaches us, "And we know that all things work together for good to them that love God, to them who are called according to his purpose." That verse is so true. I was finally healed from the pain of losing my father, because another one was given to me. Not just any man but a loving, Christian family man who stepped right into an empty place in my heart.

I miss Dad immensely, but his legacy will long live within me. God healed my pain of not having a father by supplying another godly one. We prayed together frequently. If we were in the same place praying, we held hands. If we were separated, we prayed over the phone. Our prayer time was special. When we prayed, we interceded on behalf of others. That reminded me of those prayer warriors that prayed for my healing so many years ago. I am grateful for them.

Dad taught me so much. Nothing is too small to take to God in prayer. If something matters to me, it matters to God. Just like with me and Dad. He impressed upon me that helping people in need is best done anonymously. Giving is not for our glory. The Bible says in Matthew 6:2-4,

> So when you give to the needy, do not announce it with trumpets, as the hypocrites do in the synagogues and on the streets, to be honored by others. Truly I tell you, they have received their reward in full. But when you give to the needy, do not let your left hand know what your right hand is doing, so that your

giving may be in secret. Then your Father, who sees what is done in secret, will reward you. KJV

I saw a lot of God shine through Dad. Dad took "steps" out of relationships and said we were all just family. He easily forgave, was always ready to offer sage advice and comfort, and changed my life for the better. This is what healed my hurt from losing my first father, Daddy. My Heavenly Father sent me another Christian one, Dad, and my heart not only healed but flourished from that blessing. I am thankful God added the extra onto my blessing.

Nyla Kay Wilkerson

Nyla Kay Wilkerson is a follower of Jesus and prayer warrior. A retired Christian bookstore owner and Sunday School teacher, she now edits, reviews books, writes Christian blogs, (abbasprayerwarriorprincess@wordpress), and co-blogs on HeartWingsBlog (heartwingsblog.com). She is a contributing writer for *Chicken Soup for the Soul* and *Guideposts*, and is writing a novel. She has published one cookbook and is working on a second one. Hobbies include writing, cooking, gardening, and reading. She is Mom to two and Gram to four. A widow, she resides in Indiana with her two pets.

5

† *For ALL Have Sinned and Fallen Short of the Glory of God…*

by Rachael Cameron

You may have heard the term "womb to the tomb" Christian. That's how one of my cousins referred to many of our extended family. We were born into Christian homes, part of a large extended family of believers, at church every Sunday, and raised to be decent moral citizens.

One of my school friends, herself from a broken home, commented that I had a "fairytale" life. It was only after graduating high school that I started to contemplate how blessed my life was, and how strange that in spite of having this beautiful life, there was a growing void within me. Yet at the same time, I felt like "being good" was so simple and something I could achieve even without God's help.

Our extended family had always been quite close, even when separated by distance. So once high school was over, I decided to book a flight to Townsville and spend a few weeks where my Nana Nell and many of my favorite cousins lived. I had a blast! I stayed at Nana's but spent much of my time with four cousins who were around my age.

It was only when it was time to book a flight home that a problem arose. I'd given my dad the cash to buy my airfare home, but he'd spent it on something else and couldn't afford to replace the money yet! I was not impressed. The news had come that I'd been accepted into the university I had planned to attend and the degree I'd planned to take, but I was mad at him. However, all of that means nothing now. He called to say he'd replace the money soon, and I could come home and start my teaching degree. But I flat refused and said I'd just stay in Townsville and go to Bible college with my cousin Steve.

That's exactly what I did. I signed up for Bible college, and was quickly immersed into a much more zealous Christianity than I'd ever before experienced. We studied, served, and worshipped week by week…but something was still missing. I started to wonder whether or not I was actually born again. My parents said I'd given my heart to the Lord as a child, but I had no real memory of that event and wondered how passing from death to life could just fade from memory like that.

I wanted God so much, but when it came to salvation and re-pentance, I couldn't really think of any obvious sins I'd com-mitted…yet still knew I was a sinner. One night, feeling very concerned that I was not really born again, I flicked through my Bible to the very back where the Sinner's Prayer was. I prayed it about three times, but I felt nothing and cried my-self to sleep in despair.

Altar calls were common at our church, like so many other churches, I'm sure. For weeks I'd been toying with the idea of responding to one. But they'd usually have a theme, and I couldn't think of how my situation fit with any of those themes! That changed one night at a Youth Service, when again, there was an altar call, but then the pastor stopped and had a word of knowledge. He said there was a young lady in the audience who had been raised in a Christian home and had been saved long ago. He went on to say this person needed to rededicate her heart to the Lord and had been feeling very dry.

"That's me," I thought. Then a voice in my head, likely God, said "Get up there." I gave it a few seconds, then felt like I was being drawn out and raced up there. Others started to follow, and before the pastor had even got over to me, the tears started flowing, and I felt a literal weight or burden lift from within me, and felt the joy and life from Jesus flowing in.

For a long time, I'd lived in self-righteousness and carried out the facade that my relationship with God was just fine. I believe that the need to respond to that public altar call, rather than just praying a sinner's prayer alone in my room, was the Lord asking me to make a public confession that I too was a sinner in need of the Savior.

Rachael Cameron

Rachael Cameron resides in sunny Queensland, Australia, where she and her family of eight are organic market gardeners. Rachael loves life as a wife and mother, serving Jesus, homeschooling, homesteading, and assisting with running the family business.

6

by Shonda Fischer

Coming from a background with mental abuse leaves you without confidence. In fact, it leaves you like a broken vessel that gets filled up with only the negative things ever said about you. I've always felt stupid, incompetent, and like I was not worth much to anyone.

We tend to see our Heavenly Father as we see our earthly father. For me it was that I was undeserving of love and acceptance. Growing up it kept me from being loved the way God wanted me to be loved. I continued looking for relationships that were similar to my relationship with my earthly father, which left me with much hurt and sorrow. As I grew into adulthood and spent more time around family, I would hear conversations about my father and his life. My father endured unimaginable hurt from his childhood. Consequently, that is why he became so angry with life and treated his children the only way he knew.

My heart broke for what my dad had endured. He was looking for unconditional love just like me. He was broken and needed healing. My father had a relationship with God, but after enduring more hurts in his adult life, he wanted nothing to do with God. Unfortunately, my dad turned his back on Him. I feel there is a pattern here! Once I gave my life to God, He began opening my eyes to things in my past that had hurt me. I recognized the hurt in my dad's life and why he acted the way he did. I knew he loved me but didn't know how to show it.

I began loving my father the way God loved me. Slowly, my relationship with my father began to change. I found myself taking my daughter to spend time with him. We would talk while I cut his hair and watched old western shows with him. My dad would invite me to come over and eat his homemade chili. I absolutely loved his chili. We were growing closer. My dad was showing a different side of himself. I found myself being healed and could see in my dad that he also was being healed by God. I actually found myself looking forward to his phone calls and spending time with him. We became close and often found ourselves talking out our problems with each other.

My father never came out and asked for forgiveness, but I think this was his way of trying to right his wrongs. After all, aren't we all broken in some way or another? Don't we need to be forgiven for things we have said or done to others because of hurt we ourselves have endured?

God was showing me how I need to forgive and understand that hurt people often hurt others. How can we begin to have healing if we aren't willing to forgive others? I asked God to forgive me and to help me let go of all my hurts. I wanted so much to have a relationship with my father and to show him that no matter what, he was forgiven and loved.

On June 27, 1996 my father passed away from a massive heart attack. I was there to see him not responding and turning blue. My heart was shattered into a million pieces. I felt it would never be made whole again. How would I ever survive this unbearable hurt?! As I poured out my heart to God, I felt peace and joy surrounding me. I was given a chance not many ever get, and was healed through God's beautiful grace.

God has forgiven me of all my sins. I grieved Him terribly when I was living in sin. He has brought me through so much; His love for me never fails. He died on the cross for me because He would rather die than spend eternity without me. I know that even if I was the only person on earth, God loves me so much He still would have chosen the cross. I now see myself through the eyes of the King!

We often choose to see ourselves as our earthly fathers see us, when we should be looking at how God sees us. He created us in His image. He gave us our gifts and talents. We are fearfully and wonderfully made, but most of all He paid the ultimate sacrifice for us by enduring suffering and hanging on a cross. I invite you to ask God to heal your hurts and give you eyes to see His amazing, wonderful love.

> Eye has not seen, nor ear heard, nor have entered into the heart of man the things which God has prepared for those who love Him.
> 1 Corinthians 2:9

Shonda Czeschin Fischer

Shonda Czeschin Fischer is a wife and mother of two, who has been married for twenty-one years to her husband, Craig. She has worked alongside him in children's ministry for seventeen years. Shonda loves reading, reviewing books, and anything involving history. She resides in Missouri, where she spends time with her ShihTzu, Daisy, and Siamese cat, Nala. Shonda loves to talk about God. She enjoys encouraging and uplifting others.

7

† *People's Lives Are Rarely What They Appear*

▼

by Sydney Tooman Betts

My family had everything. My father was a vice president of a worldwide company, my mother a sought-after beauty, and my only sibling a great academic success. The view from inside the family was different. My father had little joy and was rarely available emotionally. My mom never seemed to gain enough adoration to satisfy her inward cravings, and one summer my sibling attempted to take his or her life.

During the next year, for me, several inner and outward strands of events wove together. I gained admittance to my school's popular crowd only to discover it held nothing I desired, and when each party ended, I was left listening alone to Peggy Lee's, "Is That All There Is?"

The song stood out. It was an odd selection for our local rock station and epitomized my feelings. After all, my family had already achieved the goals everyone told me were worth pursuing, and yet they had nothing.

God, who knows the secret longings of our hearts, can use anything—even petty sibling rivalry. While climbing the stairs, I overheard Mom asking Dad, "Did you know [sibling's name] reads the Bible for half an hour a day?" So, what did I do? I said to myself, "Ha! I will read it an hour a day!" I did, but it brought up a host of questions for which I had no answers.

I was the family good kid, but compared with the standards I read in the Gospels, I was far from measuring up. When I read Mark 8:38, "Whoever is ashamed of me...the Son of Man will be ashamed of when He returns...," I knew I was in trouble. What was I to do? The thought of carrying a Bible to school filled my fifteen-year-old heart with dread, and try as I might, I could not stop sassing my mother. That was clearly not a way to show her honor. I truly struggled to be good from the heart, as Jesus described, but I failed miserably. The standard was just impossible.

Then came the summer I met a handsome pastor's son who introduced me to philosophy and Buddhism. Maybe, he proposed, I only believed in Jesus because my parents said He was real—sort of like Santa Claus, and we all know how that turned out. I had almost convinced myself he was right, but then I remembered a couple of events from my younger days.

The first happened while I was in our parochial school, listening to our teacher read the Bible. I felt a palpable presence I now recognize as the Holy Spirit. The second was when I was about eleven years old. A friend of my grandmother's took me to a healing service. The evangelist's sermon was far over my head, but I watched as he prayed for a man's leg to grow to match the length of his other one—and it did! While I could cast my earlier experience as imagination, what was I to do with a leg growing directly before my eyes? We had great seats.

Next, one sunny afternoon while reading my handsome mentor's philosophy assignment, my mind wandered to the

Psalms I'd been reading. David expressed himself to a God that was far more personal and involved than the one I envisioned. I thought of Him as a distant authority figure, much like my high school principal, available mainly to punish. I wanted David's God and told Him so, promising I would follow Him for the rest of my life provided that He make Himself as real to me as He had to David. He did!

Right then and there, my heart was changed, and I rejoiced in the filling of it. I wanted to carry my Bible to school and wanted to talk about Him to anyone who would listen, not out of duty but wonder. As He faithfully wooed me through His Word, He gave me beauty for ashes and a garment of praise. He has never failed me yet.

Sydney Tooman Betts

Sydney Tooman Betts resides near the cavern system that inspired parts of her book *Light Bird's Song*.

Ms. Betts' (B.S. Bible/Missiology, M.Ed) teaching experiences span early childhood to guest lecturing at the graduate level, but her favorite subject is the Word of God.

Before penning her first novel, *A River too Deep*, she ghostwrote several stories for an adult literacy program.

8

♡ *Enduring Friendship*

▼

by Samuel Stewart

Am I alone? I have asked myself this many times, just as countless people throughout history have. Descartes asked this when he wondered if there was a world outside of his own mind. Copernicus was originally opposed and had to look for others to agree with him that the Earth orbited the sun, rather than the opposite. George Washington may have felt in Valley Forge that he was the only one who truly believed in democracy. In my case, I was the kid on the playground, sitting in solitude by the door, waiting for recess to end.

It is true that I have been blessed with having a loving, Christian family that has always been there for me. I am also an introvert, which means most of the time being alone doesn't bother me. However, no matter what personality type one is, everyone needs and desires human connection. As I grew up and learned about the world, I strengthened my faith in God. In addition to my family, I knew I wasn't existentially alone either, although I still had that friendship-shaped hole in my heart.

When I was twelve years old and in seventh grade, the Spirit moved in my heart, and I began fervently studying Scripture. The plan I used directed me to I John. I read in the fifth chapter that God will listen when we ask for things that are according to His will. I asked Him for a friend. Of course, I meant a real friend, someone who wants to spend time together, is loyal, and can be there in time of need. Interestingly, a classmate of mine named John, whom I had known for years, asked me later that day if I wanted to play tennis with him.

John and I played tennis many times after that and grew very close. His family even took me along on their vacation once! I finally had a good friend. As I went through high school, there was one period that I found very challenging. Social circles were awkward, and academics were demanding as well as challenging. Several mornings I woke up feeling exhausted. I questioned what the meaning of my life was. I'm not sure I have an answer for that yet, but what kept me going during that season was looking forward to the next time I got to hang out with John.

My church's youth group provided a very welcoming and encouraging environment that helped me come out of my shell. Whether it was discussing theology or playing games, two friends named Taylor and Alex proved to have more staying power than the rest. I now had a threefold answer to prayer. Alex even became my roommate during our first and fourth years at Wheaton College in Illinois.

During that first year, we became close with our two neighbors, Steve and Matthew, in addition to enjoying the camaraderie that the group on our quirky floor provided. One day during the winter, a dozen of us went skiing. At one point I got separated from the group and felt lost. I prayed to the Lord asking for direction and to reunite quickly with my friends. In that moment I realized that even if my friends were not with me, the Lord, with whom I had grown close, would still be there as my True Friend. (I did soon find my friends, and all was well that day.)

I felt more accepted and included than ever before in my life. Not only did I have several friends to call my own, but I was also a member of a group. I was grateful for sure, but somehow my heart that had for so long only desired one friend could not be satisfied. I did not think that this was enough. Alex and our two neighbors lived together with John and Tyler (other friends from the floor) the next year. I decided to live with two others, thinking I should form my own friendships and not rely on those I shared with someone I had known before college. What I have learned since then is that sharing a good thing does not make it any less good. This decision created (or perhaps simply revealed) great insecurity in me, which I struggled with for some time afterward.

Though I remained friends with everyone I have mentioned, I thought for the first time that I might lose some of the friends, as they grew closer to each other. I felt unnecessary. One late night in the very first week of the year, I just sat down in the dorm hallway before reaching my room and cried for a while. It was as though I made a mistake and all my sadness was my own fault, which I still believe is true. I was fortunate enough to have options of which friends to live with, but for some reason this fact was completely lost on me at the time, due to jealousy.

Life went on as it tends to do, and I became very close friends with one of the guys I had chosen to live with that year, Josh. Had I made a different decision, that connection may not have ever happened, especially since he was (and still is) a very busy man. Despite good coming from the situation,

I only learned that in hindsight. My insecurities continued to grow. The next year we all moved into apartments. A group of twelve of us split into three groups of four. Two groups were very close to each other, but mine was in a different complex. This time it was not my doing, but I again ended up with the short stick, feeling distanced from the group.

One night in the middle of winter, as I was walking back from the main group to my apartment, I wondered why I struggled through difficult academics and sacrificed sleep for friends that I felt did not need me. I was feeling alone again, that familiar feeling. This time it was deeper, because rather than the status quo, it was unwelcome and resembled a sense of loss. I felt removed from my new friends, as well as from my family, John, and Taylor. I had not seen them in months.

As I came upon the railroad tracks that crossed campus between the two apartment complexes, I wondered if anyone would care if I were gone. A horn sounded as a train approached. My family and friends all had other family and friends to care for them. Was I really necessary? John did tell me once that he didn't know what he would do without me. I decided to continue on after the train passed. Besides, I couldn't make a life-altering decision that late at night, at least not without contemplating it seriously after a full night of sleep! Once again, that first answer to prayer was a blessing in my life.

I never seriously considered those dark thoughts when the sun was up, and I never gave much credence to them beyond my insecurities. Senior year of college finally arrived. Twelve of us were blessed to have one of the few coveted on-campus houses. On the first floor, I was with the five I declined to join previously. Colby and Brian were among those upstairs. Living with all those I had become close to during college was a blessing, and I think that year was the best year of my life.

In the four and a half years since graduating from college, I have grown to accept peace with my relationships. No friendship will ever be as close as my relationship with the Lord. Friends enjoying other friendships do not render mine any less meaningful or diminish their value. I have only grown closer to my early friends John and Taylor and have remained close with those I grew near to in college. Plus, I have even met some new faces, which becomes less intimidating with each new season of life. I have been blessed with a more loving family, more quality friendships, and a deeper relationship with God than I could have ever imagined when I was sitting by myself, staring at the playground, and wondering what it felt like to be included.

Now, I rarely ask myself the original question: Am I alone? The answer for me is a resounding no. There is an inexplicable healing that comes from that realization. For this I am eternally grateful. Thanks be to God!

Samuel Stewart

My name is Samuel Stewart, and my home is in Wisconsin. I am a follower of Jesus who has a passion for understanding the world. I studied math and economics at Wheaton College in Illinois and now work in the financial industry, of course in addition to my writing.

9

† *God Softened My Heart*

▼

by Latisha Sexton

I have always felt that my testimony of coming to Christ was boring. My life, according to the world, was not in chaos or despair. In fact, my life was pretty good. The fact that I was a "good girl" and wasn't struggling with what are considered by most to be major sins (drugs, sexual relationships outside of marriage, etc.) has for years made me second guess my salvation.

However, as I have grown in my faith and knowledge of Christ, I have come to realize that it doesn't matter. Just because my life wasn't a total wreck to the world does not mean that I was righteous or holy. I was still a hopeless sinner that needed to repent and believe in Jesus to save me from my own wickedness.

Let me start from the beginning. I was raised in church from the time that I was born and have always believed in God (but then again, even the devil believes, right?). However, I was young and didn't fully grasp my own sinfulness or that I was doomed to an eternity in hell, unless Christ called me and drew me to Himself.

The year before repenting and truly believing in Christ, I experienced a lot of anxiety. I feared death down to my core. I remember being too terrified to go to sleep, not knowing where I would end up if I died. I prayed *the* prayer over and over, but the fear remained, lodging deep in my soul. I carried around a heavy weight of guilt. You see, I was praying and using the words that I was "supposed" to say. But I wasn't believing it in my heart. However, God was definitely using this time to soften my heart to Him and His Word. I read my Bible almost daily, trying to find something that would bring me peace.

When I was eleven years old, I was listening to a song on my portable CD player (yes, I am that old). I don't remember who the artist was or even the song, but I do recall it was a song about death and hell. I remember the overwhelming guilt. My chest was so heavy, and I was near tears. It was then that I knew that I was a sinner and my sins alone were enough to put Jesus on that Cross.

I told my mom that I wanted to talk. She asked me questions and prayed along with me. That was the moment that Jesus drew me to Him, and I surrendered my heart and life to Him. I didn't feel an immediate "magical" feeling, but the tension and heaviness in my chest eased off. I knew that this time, the prayer and my heart were different.

I still struggled a lot during those early years as a new believer. I struggled with jealousy, pride, and idols in my life. The difference was that I had the Holy Spirit to convict me of these things and help me to overcome them through His power. At the time, I didn't realize how much coming to Christ at a young age had changed the course of my life. As an adult woman, with a husband and three small children, I can see that the decisions I made as a young Christian brought me to this place. I can see the mistakes that others my age made, and I know that without Jesus in my life during those times, I would have followed right along with them. Because I am not better than anyone else, I have the same sinful desires in my heart. Only Christ in me has given me the power to overcome these temptations and avoid the heartaches that so many others have had early on in life.

I pray for anyone reading this, that you would know that you don't have to have the most shocking testimony in the world because the angels in heaven rejoice when even one sinner enters the fold. No matter how "small" your sins may seem, your testimony is powerful. Your testimony is a witness to the powerful mercy and grace of our Lord Jesus Christ.

Latisha Sexton

My name is Latisha Sexton. I am foremost a follower of Christ. I have been happily married for twelve years to my soulmate. He and I have three children together, ages six, five, and three years old. My journey has been a very long one, but God has guided each and every step. I am able to look back and see that He has brought me to this…becoming an author and writer.

10

 God's Journey for Us to Our Rainbow Baby

by Samantha Gilson

(Written on the due date of our baby that miscarried)

Today is a hard day. Today, my husband, Ian, and I were supposed to become Mommy and Daddy for the first time. We were supposed to be holding our sweet first baby and introducing them to our friends and family. However, God had other plans, and our sweet little Nugget gets to spend their due date with Him. I cannot be too upset because I know we are having the baby we are supposed to have in our sweet rainbow baby Miss Eva Kate (who we are super excited to welcome in September), but I can't help missing our first little Nugget! I am glad they did not have to experience any pain, and I am glad they continue to teach me that God can heal all hurts! We love you, our sweet Nugget, and we know you are getting loved and snuggled up in heaven. Happy Due Date, sweet baby!

Our Miscarriage Story
(some graphic and difficult details included, please be warned before reading, this is not for everyone)

In May/June 2020, Ian and I decided we were ready to start trying to grow our family (with more than just fur babies). I went off birth control, and in July I had my yearly check up and got the okay to start trying. At the end of July 2020, I had what would be my last true period for over a year. In August, I missed my period (I am never late). We had a positive pregnancy test and were so excited! I made a doctor's appointment for a week and a half later (that was the soonest I could get in), but the following Friday I started bleeding. At the emergency room it was determined that I most likely had a chemical pregnancy (egg and sperm meet but do not implant). And with that, we lost our first pregnancy.

It didn't hit me super hard because we hadn't known for long, we hadn't even gotten a chance to nickname them, and that baby really never had any chance to grow since it had not implanted. We were given the go ahead to try again immediately and in September, we again had a positive test! We were so excited again, albeit a bit more hesitant. We made it to the first doctor's appointment, and they confirmed I was pregnant. October brought an ultrasound, and they determined the baby was six weeks along but couldn't detect a heartbeat yet. They had us come back one week later, and at seven weeks gestation we got to hear our sweet Nugget's heartbeat and see them on the ultrasound! We fell in love with our sweet little baby. We told some friends and family in person but decided not to post anything online until we were out of the first trimester.

For a month after that we made plans! We bought baby stuff, collected hand me downs, started working on the nursery, and truly began preparing for a baby. Then in November, I went for a routine check up. It was still a bit early to hear a heartbeat with a Doppler, but they went ahead and tried anyway. They couldn't find it but they said that is normal until about 12-14 weeks. They had me wait a bit so they could do a quick ultrasound. I hadn't brought anyone with me because there wasn't supposed to be an ultrasound; it was just a regular check up. But when they got the picture pulled up the tech was super confused. She saw the sac but…no baby. At some point between the seven week ultrasound and then, our Nugget had passed away, and my body had absorbed any evidence. Of course we were devastated. There had been nothing unusual, no bleeding, no cramping, nothing that would indicate we had lost the pregnancy. How does a baby just disappear?

Our wonderful mothers drove down immediately and spent the weekend with us. We cried, and mourned the loss of our sweet Nugget. We told our friends and family who had already known about the pregnancy, and they mourned too. The hardest was the nieces. How do you explain to ones so little something so hard? But Hadley put it best "Nugget is in heaven and Granny (Ian's grandmother) is holding them, and we will see them again one day." But it wasn't over yet. We got a second opinion just to be sure, and the doctor confirmed that they could still see the gestational sac, but that it had not grown, and there was no baby inside. I still can't quite wrap my head around that, how can a baby just disappear?

We were given the option to go ahead and have a D&C or wait and let my body pass the tissue naturally. We elected to wait. My body didn't register the loss for another few weeks and just after Thanksgiving I actually started to bleed. And I bled and bled, I passed huge clots, and finally I got so pale and weak and was in so much pain that Ian took me to the hospital. They checked me out and again gave me the option to have a D&C or finish waiting it out. At this point the worst was over, and we thought it was all almost out anyway so we again waited. They had me come in a week later just to double check that everything had passed and it had not, so they had to schedule a D&C after all. On December 10th I had the D&C. We were told to wait two weeks before "special hugging," and they preferred for me to have a period before earnestly trying for another baby.

Well, God had other plans (as He usually does), and on January 10th, exactly one month from the D&C I still hadn't had a period. I took a test and it was positive! I went ahead, scheduled an appointment, and took another test on the 14th just to be sure, and all turned out great! We were expecting our little peanut who is now our sweet Eva Kate! And I still hadn't had a period.

We told our family and even were able to tell my Nana before she passed. God healed our hearts through our sweet rainbow baby! We will always love and miss our sweet Nugget, and our nameless first baby who we barely knew, but we are so blessed to have our happy, healthy little baby in our arms for this difficult anniversary. It was just about this time last year that I heard the words "there's no baby." I cannot describe the confusion and pain I felt that day, and the month to follow, as we dealt with the aftermath. But God knew we needed this baby at this time! He had it all worked out, and all I had to do was trust that His plan was better than anything I could have worked out for myself. His Glory is the goal! Always! And we are so thankful for the support of our wonderful family and the gift of our most perfect baby girl. We will always love you nameless, Nugget and Eva Kate Gilson!

Epilogue: (Written when Eva Kate was four months old)
Wow, I did not realize how true this would become. God has continued to heal our hearts through our love for Him, our love for our sweet rainbow baby, and our love for each other!

These months have been nothing short of an absolute blessing! He has blessed us with a wonderful family who supports us however we need. He has given me a wonderful new job that I absolutely love and has allowed me to spend all day every day with my sweet girl. God truly provides!

I hope that you will allow God into your heart and feel His love so that He may heal your hurts from the inside out! Hurting people do hurt people, and if you are tired of hurting people or feeling hurt by others just know God can heal all hurts! He can and will heal you if you give Him your time and attention and allow Him to rule in your heart!

Samantha Gilson

Samantha is a math/chemistry teacher and cheer/dance coach from Kentucky. She currently lives in Alabama with her husband, daughter, dogs, and cat. In her free time (which is not much with a new baby), you will find her reading, in the sun, or swimming. Samantha joined the CWC to share the stories of God working in her life in hopes that they may help/inspire others as they demonstrate His love and grand plan.

11

✝ *The Thorn in the Flesh*

by L.E. McNeese

And lest I should be exalted above measure by the abundance of the revelations, a thorn in the flesh was given to me, a messenger of Satan to buffet me, lest I be exalted above measure. Concerning this thing I pleaded with the Lord three times that it might depart from me. And He said to me, "My grace is sufficient for you, for My strength is made perfect in weakness." Therefore most gladly I will rather boast in my infirmities, that the power of Christ may rest

upon me. Therefore I take pleasure in infirmities, in reproaches, in needs, in persecutions, in distresses, for Christ's sake. For when I am weak, then I am strong.
2 Corinthians 12:7-10

On December 9, 2021, I attempted suicide. I am writing this exactly two weeks later. I was in so much pain, more pain than I thought I could handle, and I wanted it to end. I had been bullied and had just lost my closest friend. I have since received help from licensed mental health providers and am currently safe, stable, and being taken care of.

A testimony is typically written as follows:

- My life before Christ

- How Jesus came into my life

- My life with Jesus

My life has been difficult, to say the least. I was never promised that it would not be. Jesus says that we will have trouble in this world, but to take heart, for He has overcome the world.

Jesus has given me the strength to endure the hardship that I face. He has allowed me to continue living this life, even when I become discouraged and am ready to give up. When I am weak, He makes me strong, and He reminds me that I can do all things through Him who strengthens me. When I feel alone, He is with me. He is with me always.

I once had a conversation with a wise older man that I shall never forget. I was struggling with self-harm at the time and went to him for advice and counsel. He shared a story with me about being in the ministry. He told me about how he has worked with lots of people, hurting and broken ones. He said that once he worked with a man struggling with alcoholism. The man told him, "I have a friend who used to drink and do drugs, and then he met Jesus and quit cold turkey. Just one day, he woke up, and decided he would be done." The man explained to him that he did not feel that way, that he still struggled with wanting to drink and fall into old patterns. He asked, heartbroken, if he had missed something.

The truth is, Jesus coming into your life radically changes it. However, it does not mean that you will be free of sin and struggle. The Christian life is one that is not easy. It is a call to daily die to self. It is a process, a journey, and a constant battle. I still struggle with feeling sad. I still struggle with feeling alone and forsaken by those who once called me a friend. I still seek help from mental health professionals when I am in dark places. And that does not make me weak or any less of a Christian. That makes me a human being in a fallen world.

My charge to you, reader, is this: keep fighting the good fight. You didn't miss anything.

L.E. McNeese

L.E. McNeese is a freshman English major at Lipscomb University in Nashville, Tennessee. She is involved with Model United Nations and her school's creative writing club. In her free time, L.E. loves attending concerts and frequenting local coffee shops. L.E. attends Covenant Presbyterian Church and is passionate about spreading the love of Christ whenever possible. She hopes that her testimony encouraged you!

12

♡ *With Jesus There Is Always More*

by Kristyn Schott

I was very fortunate growing up in that I had a fairly uneventful life in terms of pain and hurt. That is, until I reached my second semester of college and began the battle with my eating disorder. That battle lasted over a year and a half and led me to experience physical, mental, emotional, relational, and especially, spiritual pain.

Giving up taking care of either of them, I put my mind and body through horrible things. I grew distant from friends and lashed out at people I loved. I shoved everything I was feeling deeper and deeper down until it buried the good in me and simply became the only part of myself I could see. Worst of all, I felt myself pull away from God. I had never felt so distant from Him. The worst part of all of this was for that year and a half, I saw nothing wrong with what I was doing or who I was.

Praise God that He had better plans for me and stopped me before I could destroy myself completely. The first stage of this healing came from an unexpected blessing in disguise—breaking my rib during one of my senior volleyball games. In that moment, I felt broken (literally and figuratively) and utterly confused with God. In His mercy, God showed me that I wasn't actually recovered or healthy. It was time to come home to Him.

From that moment on, I began to seek God, resting and healing in so many ways. Jesus healed my hurt, simply by never giving up on me. He was always waiting patiently with open arms for me to turn to Him, over and over again. As I sought God more, He showed me more of who I was in Him and what He created me to be and do. I no longer was defined by my eating disorder but by the God who created me. It was an amazing feeling.

Surprisingly, my healing was not done. Years after I broke my rib and Jesus brought me out of my eating disorder, I still found myself struggling with similar issues or thoughts, though thankfully they were not as extreme and consuming as earlier. I was still frustrated, because hadn't Jesus healed me? Shouldn't I be done with all of this?

I don't know about you, but I'm the kind of person who wants things to be done in my timing, which usually means quickly. I'm often impatient, especially when in the middle of an uncomfortable or undesirable state. Slowly but surely, I'm learning that God's timing truly is perfect. Just because my healing takes a bit longer, doesn't mean there is anything wrong with me or God.

Here's my encouragement to you: Jesus can heal your hurt…even if it takes a bit longer.

When I started to get super frustrated by my continued struggles, God pointed me back to Jesus healing the blind man in Mark 8, starting in verse 22. People had brought a blind man to Jesus to be healed, so Jesus took this man by the hand and led him outside the village. After Jesus spat on the man's eyes and put His hands on him, He asked, "Do you see anything?"

The blind man replied, "I see people; they look like trees walking around."

So, Jesus once again placed His hands on the man's eyes and "then his eyes were opened, his sight was restored, and he saw everything clearly" (v. 25).

The first thing I noticed in this story is that Jesus took the man outside of his comfort or safe area. Imagine being the blind man and letting this stranger lead you away from the only area you've ever known. That's exactly what Jesus did, because He knew that healing involves stepping out of our comfort zone and stepping forward in faith.

The second thing is the way Jesus healed the man—spitting on his eyes, which was probably not what the blind man expected at all and just a little uncomfortable. That's because when Jesus is healing or working a miracle, it's often not comfortable or what we expected.

The final thing is, in my opinion, the most important. It's the fact that the man wasn't fully healed the first time. In fact, he stayed to receive the full healing that was waiting for him in Jesus. It would've been so easy for the man to think that receiving some sight was "good enough" compared to having no sight and just go home. However, the man stayed, because he knew and believed Jesus had more for him. His faith healed him, and Jesus fully restored his sight.

Because the truth is, with Jesus, there is always more, but we have to stay to receive it. Partial vision stops full faith, which leads to only partial healing. You see, Jesus can and does heal us. Oftentimes, we've been struggling with that hurt for so long that there are residual parts buried deep down that God has to uncover and remove from our hearts over time. There is further healing God wants to give you. He also wants to lead you to more freedom, but that takes time.

There was nothing wrong with the man or Jesus for the healing to take a second time (and there's nothing wrong with you if it takes a second, third, seventh, or whatever time for healing either). Instead, God used that moment to build and strengthen the blind man's faith, and it's ultimately that faith that healed him.

Since God has healed the bulk of my hurt by bringing me out of my eating disorder and the dark place I was stuck in, I now walk in freedom. My life now has hope, life, and peace. I am able to bring current and future dark parts of my heart into the light of Jesus, as I surrender my battles to Him. I wouldn't wish my eating disorder on my worst enemy, but I also wouldn't change going through it. It was only by going through that hurt that God was able to lead me to this place of being closer to, and on fire for, Him. Only by having Jesus lead me through the hurt, did I find the faith that enabled Him to heal me from my hurt.

We can see something similar in Mark 5:34 and Mark 10:52. In both of these verses, Jesus tells the people He has just healed that their faith has healed them.

In other words, Jesus is the healer, but it's our faith that enables the healing in our lives. Jesus can heal your hurt, but it will probably take longer than you want, be uncomfortable in the moment, and look different than you expected. That's okay, because God is doing something in the middle of the waiting, discomfort, and unmet expectations. One day, Jesus will look upon you and say: "Go, your faith has healed you."

Kristyn Schott

Hey y'all, I'm Kristyn—an author, copywriter, and founder of Created for More ministry from the great state of Texas. My goal in life is to help people take hold of faith, pursue purpose, and become all they were created to be in God. In my free time, I love to read, play the piano, and spend time with friends and family.

13

 From Tragedy to Self-Indulgence to Christ

by *Adena Czeschin*

Today I find myself reminiscing on my life and the tragic incidents which brought me back home to my roots in Christ. In 2008 my life was turned upside down from a husband who sexually abused our child to an awakening of truth from friends and family about my significant other. Validation of his promiscuity between men and women was confirmed by multiple individuals within our community. My life had shattered as, one by one, things around me kept falling. It was at that point I became angry with Christ and turned my back for what became a rough ten years, not only for me but for the three young children I was left to raise alone.

Multiple trials and tribulations surfaced as I ran from everything around me while building a wall around my heart. I was running to prevent any more pain. The misery (which kept building) found no release but did manage to welcome a new self-induced destruction. Intense nights of alcohol and fornication with a married man soon became my outlet. Chaos in my household was amplified by my newfound escape. My youngest child, who was still at home, gave me a run for my money through verbal abuse towards me and defiance towards any rules I tried to set in place. She despised me. My other two daughters failed to have anything to do with me. I was not allowed to see my grandchildren or participate with their families in any way. My life was in shambles. I was empty and always blaming everyone else for it being in such disarray. I had finally reached my breaking point. It was at that moment I decided to take my mom up on her offer and attend church with her on Sunday morning.

My mom (who was adamant with her walk in Christ) had always made sure my sister and I attended Sunday School and

Children's Church. As an adult, her invitation to church or her cliché of "leave it in God's hands and pray about it" was always ringing in my ear. Her constant prayers for me and my family were never ending. They were finally answered the day I attended services with her for the first time in ten years. Like the Prodigal Son, I had found my way back to Christ. I began attending services with her regularly, and occasionally my youngest would attend as well. My life was starting to change. The running had subsided, my heart was beginning to open, and for the first time in ten years I started to become the mom and daughter I once was.

As everyone does, I still struggle at times with the enemy who always tries to disrupt my path; however, my feet are firmly planted in my Father, the Lord Jesus Christ. His overwhelming wonder never ceases to amaze me. He always guides me in every aspect of my life and never fails to answer me. I have no fear or worry because I know when I pray, my amazing God has it. His arms will always embrace me, and His love and peace will always fill my soul. He is my rock and my salvation. It is through Him, in a world of chaos, I will shine and be a guiding light to others.

Adena Czeschin

I am Adena, a forty-nine-year-old grandma to many blessings and a warrior mother of three girls. My hobbies include music, plus a passion for helping others find their smile in Jesus Christ. This passion led me to my devoted husband Eric of two years. It is an honor to be part of the CWC fellowship.

14

 Sticks and Stones

by Kim Patterson

"Sticks and stones may break my bones, but words will never hurt me." Some injuries cut us. Some injuries break us. Some injuries even bruise us. They may not necessarily be seen from the outside, yet they still hurt especially when you press on them. This is exactly how some words that have been spoken wound us. Proverbs 18:21 tells us that the tongue has the power of life and death. Consequently, with our words we wield either an instrument of encouragement or a weapon of destruction.

I wish more parents understood this. I especially wish my parents understood this. The things that are said to children so carelessly, to minds that are not mature, can be so harmful to their emotional development and leave lasting scars. Have you ever tried to heal a scar? It takes a very long time. They don't go away instantly.

When I was young, my mom said some things that she thought would comfort me, trying to bring some reason for why my parents were divorcing and why my dad was moving to another state. Things like, "We got pregnant with you, so we had to get married. Your father never wanted a family. His work has always been more important. He wanted a boy and blamed me that I couldn't give him one." These words were all meant to justify why my dad did what he did, but what I heard was, "You were a mistake. You were unwanted. You are not important and a disappointment."

My mom did not say these things out of anger toward me or hatred for me. No, in fact, I knew she loved me, and she was trying to shift the blame to my father. However, here is what the enemy does. He takes words and twists them from their intended purpose and turns them into a lie, and we tend to believe that lie. Not only do we believe it but repeat it over and over in our head. It is like a broken record playing until it is ingrained into our thought process. Eventually the lie becomes part of our identity.

I thought this is who I was and spent so many years trying to become worthy of love through performance. I became defensive in any criticism. Criticism was just more words pressing on an open wound. Without healing, the enemy can continue to injure us. He doesn't even need to get creative, because the same thing works every time.

When we get hurt physically, sometimes what we do is put a bandage over it. What do you do with an injury to the soul? We can apply the blood of Jesus to it. For every lie that is spoken, we can cover it with the Truth. Jesus said in John 14:6, "I am the Way, the Truth, and the Life." Jesus is the Way to our healing by being the Truth over the lie, thus bringing Life to where the enemy tried to bring death. The enemy comes only to steal, kill, and destroy, but Jesus came that we may have life and have it more abundantly (John 10:10).

I began to apply the Truth to my wounds. Truths that said, "I am fearfully and wonderfully made and God has plans and a purpose for my life." Other truths such as "I am loved by

Jesus who gave His life for me, being a child of God is enough, and I can rest in Him" all chased away the lies.

The truth that set me free from the lies of the enemy is, "Jesus can heal your hurts when you know Him as Truth and apply that truth to your wounds, which gives you the power to change the narrative in your head." I made a decision to stop playing the old record and sing a new song. That choice is available to everyone, and we have to exercise the freewill that God gave us.

> Today I have given you the choice between life and death, between blessings and curses. Now I call on heaven and earth to witness the choice you make. Oh, that you would choose life, so that you and your descendants might live!
> Deuteronomy 30:19

I don't know about you, but I no longer find comfort in licking the wounds of the past. It used to be that one wrong word was like a finger pressing on an old bruise but not anymore. I have chosen life. You see, if we don't let Jesus heal us from our hurts, others will suffer, especially our children. Have you heard the expression, "Hurt people hurt people"? I don't want to be someone who hurts others because of the hurts I've experienced. I want to be someone who brings encouragement to others, having the power to release life with the words I use. As a parent, I have the power to release that to my children so that they can release it to theirs, because loved people love people. Jesus has healed me from the pain of words that wound. With His Truth, He has shown me the way to life, not only for myself, but for my descendants.

My oldest son, at a very young age, reminded me of a line from the movie, *Spider Man*. He said, "With great power comes great responsibility." The tongue holding the power of life and death is a great responsibility. How, therefore, shall we choose to exercise that responsibility? From a place of hurt and woundedness, I hurt and wounded others with my words. Subsequently, from a place of healing and wholeness provided by Jesus, my words release life. I pray you will choose life today.

Kim Patterson

Kim Patterson is a wife and mother of three. She has been a leader in her church for the past thirteen years, leading various small groups and teaching Bible studies. Kim has a passion for women's ministries and discipleship. It is her love for the Lord that fuels her desire to see others grow in Christ and walk in freedom and victory.

15

† *God's Work in Everyday Life*

by Helen Brown

Both my parents were committed Christians all of their lives, so being born to these parents, who were both very good examples of how to walk in the way Jesus wants us to go, was a privilege. In one sense it was an advantage, but it also made it hard for me to determine when exactly I became a Christian. I remember coming home for lunch one day, during fifth year of schooling, and telling Mum that I had made a decision to follow Jesus personally. However, if you were to ask me for a date and time, I couldn't pin it down. I always believed that God would lead me into ministry, just as my parents were. He has, but it's a very different looking ministry.

Did my life change dramatically after that lunchtime confession of faith? No, not really; however, all through my life I have walked through green valleys and dry places, and the Holy Spirit has been there with me every step of the way. The green valleys were times when I could see the Holy Spirit doing special things in my life, such as being part of an outreach organization at High School, my first year away from home working and having fellowship with new Christian friends, during the birth of my second daughter, and when I started writing for our church bulletin, which looking back, was the start of my writing journey and ministry through books.

My marriage to a farmer in 1978 meant that my life took a path that would teach me many varied lessons about unconditional love, perseverance, tolerance, and using His imagination to train and care for the five children that God gave us, each one with different health and personality challenges. He does His most powerful work through me every day, helping me to get out of bed, when I don't feel I want to, when I am aching all over, and when I'm depressed and I don't want to face the stress of farming life. He helps me do things around the farm, giving extra strength and courage when I need it. It's in the mundane things of life, where I see His most powerful work. It is these experiences that form the basis of my stories.

Sometimes I still struggle with my calling, my ministry. I dreamed of being a preacher like my parents, instead, I have been called to minister through written words. My first book came about almost accidentally. It was a series of stories written for the church bulletin and used as encouragement for others. When I realized that I had written enough for a book, I decided it was time. After this I kept writing, and the books kept coming. In 2019, my daughter and I started our own publishing group as it was becoming too expensive to publish externally. While I still wonder what God is doing, I know that He has blessed people through, not only my books, but the other books we have published as well.

Helen Brown

Born in Australia to Salvation Army parents, who later became Presbyterian, Helen Brown lives on a farm. The struggles of raising five children and being a wife to a shearer/farmer in a small town taught her a lot about life and the grace of God. It is this that inspires her writing. When she isn't working on the farm, she enjoys knitting, gardening, reading, and teaching.

16

♡ *Your Head Is Not as Hard as You Think*

▼

by Ruth Ann Gumm

Monday morning—I am so excited about a new video server for the live stream, BCHS Live! in my High School class. Really, I think I am more excited than the students.

Monday afternoon—Hooked it up, but I am not happy with the quality of output. Hmmm, how is all of this connected? Coming back from behind the BCHS Live! setup, I hit my head squarely on the sharp corner of our broadcasting shelf.

The shelf is mounted on a concrete wall that did not give at all. I knew immediately that I had done more damage than a simple "noggin knock" but had no idea how much damage I actually had done.

Like we all do when we hit our heads, my hand raised to my scalp to assess the damage. I soon felt the trickle of blood between my fingers and knew this wasn't going to be a simple accident. I heard co-workers saying the obligatory "Are you okay?" from the next room. I replied simply, "I'm not sure yet."

With a bottle of "new skin" and the help of the school nursing instructor, we got the bleeding stopped.

Tuesday morning—students asked me the process to troubleshoot a network drop. This is a detailed procedure but one I have done hundreds of times over the last twenty years of running a student technology help desk. The pain was so bad trying to process my thoughts that I started to cry. Trying to process thoughts HURT! Something was seriously wrong.

Later that morning I drove my ninety-year-old mother to have her pacemaker checked. She kept telling me that she could tell I was "not thinking right." When I took her home, she made me call my doctor. My mother explained to me how to get to my doctor's office because I couldn't remember. Thankfully, I made it safely. They diagnosed me with a brain injury. Their instructions were to go home, rest, and not go back to work until Monday.

Trying to process thoughts was physically painful! When I tried to think through anything, it hurt on the right side of my head over my ear and on the left side toward the front. The nerd in me thought the sections of the brain that hurt with specific tasks was really cool! (I said the nerd in me . . . stop judging! lol)

If I heard people fussing on TV, the left back side of my head hurt. Trying to process new information caused pain in the dead center of my head, then it felt like my brain short circuited and felt numb.

This experience continued through Wednesday, Thursday, Friday, and Saturday.

On Friday, the right carotid artery in my neck was painful. On Saturday night at 11:30 p.m., I felt pain and tenderness in the back of my head, neck, and shoulders. There was intense RINGING IN MY EARS, loud to the point of not being able to hear conversation.

My husband, Steve, asked, "Do you need to go to the ER?" My answer was, "I don't know. If I'm not better in the morning, I think it will be necessary." The honest answer was that I felt too bad to get dressed to go to the hospital. Throughout this process, I repeated prayers for God to show me what was happening to me. I questioned Him, "God, how much worse is this going to get?"

Next is where this story gets REALLY GOOD and RE-ALLY GOD!

Sunday 7:00 am—I wake up, still feel terrible, decided, yes, I need to go to the ER when Steve awakes.

7:13 am—I receive a random text from my Aunt Carolyn: "How r u? It's been quite a week for prayer! The leader of the group going to Israel, her husband is miraculously recovering from heart issues. The legacy of intercession is what I want to leave. Oneness with the Trinity that moves mountains!"

At that moment, I felt an urging of the Holy Spirit saying, "My child, you haven't asked ME to heal you yet." I, being me, argued, "Yes I have." "No" this overwhelming essence continued, "You have asked me 'How bad is this?' You have asked me 'Do I need a doctor?' 'When will I get better?' But you haven't asked Me to heal you." Now humbled, I replied,

"You're right . . . I haven't." Then I prayed, "God, you knit me together in my mother's womb. You knew me before I became a being. You have loved me for all time. You can heal me. I realize this will be simple for you. God, I ask you to heal me now, and I accept your healing of my brain."

I began to immediately feel better, but at the same time I was questioning what I was experiencing. "Could this be real? Could healing really be this simple?"

The moment my doubting mind finally gave over to the FACT that God was healing my brain, I felt warm, and electrified tingles were permeating throughout my brain. There was a physical manifestation of synapsis re-closing and neurons re-firing throughout the inside of my skull. It felt like a motion graphic from a sci-fi movie where you can visualize electrodes firing through the circuitry of the human brain. It was beautiful, supernatural, warm, and loving. There was no pain, just healing. Immediately there was no pain in thought.

The only lingering symptom is a ringing in my ears. I believe that may be a permanent "thorn in the flesh" gift to remind me of God's healing touch on February 23, 2020.

Ruth Ann Gumm

Ruth Ann is mother to two lovely young women, mother-in-love to two amazing men, and bonus mom to beautiful twin daughters. She is a retired technology teacher, cheerleading coach, and FBLA (Future Business Leaders of America) sponsor. She continues to help with the FCA (Fellowship of Christian Athletes) group that she co-sponsored while an educator. Her interests include her precious grandchildren, who have captured her heart, her many miniature dogs, cooking, softball, gardening, and teaching Bible Study. Her heart is especially fond of the Guatemalan people who she serves annually on a medical mission. She is an active member of her church. Along with her husband, Steve, Ruth Ann resides in the Commonwealth of Kentucky.

17

† *God Offers True Comfort*

▼

by Tracy Van Dolder

An unhurried embrace, a shoulder to cry on, a long conversation, time spent together in comfortable silence—these and many others are images of how people comfort each other. When we are feeling lonely or sad, comfort can help us get through it. The word "comfort" has a sense of closeness, a type of intimacy with someone in a time of sadness.

When my uncle passed away, I was heartbroken, but it wasn't just because my family had lost him. During the months leading up to his death, many in my family had joined our faith and believed, beyond the shadow of any doubt, that he would recover from his declining health and live. We waited for positive updates, and even when the negative ones came, we continued believing that it was only a matter of time. The more he declined, the more sure I became.

Then the news came: My uncle had died. Bizarrely, I did not stand down. Instead, I prayed for his resurrection and shut up any doubts I had. God is our healer; He would not disappoint us!

The minutes turned to hours, then days. Around the fourth day, I felt a sense that it was time to let go, but I continued to believe, quietly, impatiently, just in case. I wanted to be able to say, "I never gave up hope!" if a resurrection miracle were to occur. I wanted to impress God with my faith. But the days dragged on, and one night, finally, I gave up. And that giving up came with a flood of tears, heartbreak, and a desperate cry to God: "Why?!"

Isn't that a question we have all posed to Him a few hundred times? If we're being honest, I think we can agree that the whys all stem from one thing: we believe God failed. We think that if we had been in control, we would have done the right thing. And when we're in that place, contentedly stuck there because we think our anger is justified, the strong temptation is to avoid God, to stop reading the Bible, and to not pray—really, to give Him the silent treatment. It's the only thing we can think of to punish Him on some level.

Friend, if you've been there or are there now, I hope you can find some solace in the knowledge that you are not alone. Your desire to be angry with God because something happened that you hate, that you wish you could undo at any cost, is understandable. But can I tell you a secret? He is the only One that will truly comfort you.

After I let go that night, I felt like I had lost something precious to me—Someone. And the temptation to give it all up was, well, tempting. But I knew that if I did that, even just for a period of time, it would be very difficult to get back on track. I knew I had to stick with it and find answers that I knew I wouldn't find anywhere but in God.

It didn't take long for me to experience His healing, but it wasn't the kind that I had expected when I prayed for healing for my uncle. Instead, God began to work on my heart. He healed my hurt through His Word, His love, and His comfort. When I mentioned those images before, I doubt you imagined God as the second party in them. It's difficult to put the God of the universe in the picture of an unhurried embrace, giving a shoulder to cry on, having a long conversation with, or spending time in comfortable silence. But I believe there is a good reason that Jesus chose the word "Comforter" to describe the Holy Spirit.

When I was feeling lost, He brought stories of Jesus to my mind, and I became obsessed with them, not knowing that, even when I was still in a place of pain, He was using those stories to show me things about Himself. He waited patiently for me to discover the hidden treasure in His Word that showed His love for me, as if He were holding me in His arms, gentle and unrushed, as I waited for the sense that I had been held long enough.

In the moments when I needed to cry because that hurt was still very real, He sat with me and let me mourn, but I was not alone. He offered me His shoulder to cry upon.

When I couldn't seem to figure out what was true, He directed me to teachings and sermons that opened my eyes to His purposes and goodness. In essence, I got to have many, many long conversations with Him as His Word was explained to me and He, through the Bible, answered my questions. The more I got to know His Word, I got to know Him, and His presence changed everything.

And during those times that I didn't feel like I had the right words to pray, I would spend time with Him in comfortable silence, knowing that He was with me and I could trust Him with my doubts.

I'm still learning. Oh, goodness, am I still learning. I long for more of His comfort, His love, and His presence in my life. But even while I learn, I know one thing for certain that will not change—He is good. And He is faithful to heal your hurt, just as He healed mine.

Tracy Van Dolder

Tracy Van Dolder is a graphic designer, writer, voice actor, and Bible enthusiast. When she isn't creating book covers for her freelance design business, she can probably be found writing movie scripts, episodes for her audio show *Witnesses*, or her first novel. Her heart's desire is to use her talents to bring others to a saving knowledge of Jesus.

18

♡ *Jesus Heals from the Inside*

▼

by Lindsey Schuler

In my life there have been many times of hurt, even with the protection of conservative values and being in love with Jesus. I tell you, with every hurt there has been a process of healing and restoration when speaking those hurts aloud to the Lord in my time alone with Him. He proves this true, time and time again:

Yet when holy lovers of God cry out to Him with all their hearts, the Lord will hear them and come to rescue them from all their troubles. The Lord is close

> to all whose hearts are crushed by pain, and He is al-
> ways ready to restore the repentant one.
> Psalm 34:17-18 (TPT)

Much of my hurt has come from relationships in the sense of caring about people deeply combined with longing for a romantic relationship in marriage that portrayed the love of Christ for people, for his church. At fifteen years old, I knew with my whole heart that I wanted and would be married someday to someone who I thought would be like-minded in beliefs, dreams for children, adoption, ministry, missions, and have a similar background to my family. My criteria was being someone who loved Jesus, had a similar sense of humor, was a certain height difference, and who understood all the things I expected of him. Those things were shallow expectations I had made up.

At that age I had a conversation in my journal between the Lord and myself which went something like this: "Jesus, I believe You have a good man and good marriage for me. I really like this guy at church" (who meets the above criteria AND has dark hair, light eyes, handsome physique). God responded: "No. This is not the man I have for you."

He continued with the promise that He placed that good desire in my heart and that if I continued to follow His lead, He would bring the right man. For that time, however, with that man He brought me to Romans 6 and Romans 8. He taught me to treat this man as a brother, to love him as a brother. I realized when I was dreaming of him often and couldn't stop myself from thinking about this man, even more than God, that there was a different problem. I was placing this man in the center of my heart and allowing myself to lust after him instead of actually surrendering all the "girl brain" feelings to the Lord. Because of this, I found my mind and actions directed toward pleasing a man for nearly seven years, a man who did not care for me in the same way. Actually, if it was not for God's goodness and wisdom of starting me in college in a different city and giving me a different focus, I don't know if I would have been well.

After a few years of college, I ended up in the same city as the man who was my friend, in spring 2015. We had the same friend group, and he became close to my best friend. After a couple more years, everyone's lives changed. My best friends just stopped being close. This hurt because I cared deeply for both of them. I know how to love a brother because I have nine brothers, and I would give my life for any of them. My best female friend became a missionary abroad.

The other people I had known at church and had lived with, all moved away. I had moved to a city of promise to be alone despite putting in effort to build friendships for when I would one day get to move there. I found myself alone except for this man.

Obviously being alone brought us closer because we would go on walks after going to the church worship nights. We talked about many things, and I shared all of my heart and dreams with him. It did not take long to be in a place mentally, emotionally, and spiritually of feeling the connection that I thought was meant to be from courting to marriage. I didn't have the courage to bring this up to him, at first.

In the fall of 2015 we went to a movie together, and the whole time I fought thoughts of lust or sexual desire. I had also paid for the movie just to spend the time with him, despite feeling internally that it was not a wise choice. After the film, he told me that he was denied other plans, and that's why he spent that time with me. I told him that we should not spend the night hours together because for me it is intimate. He agreed. After that I did not hear from him for a month, despite my calling him when my sister's family was saved from a fire. Her church had burned down, and she was in the parish at the time. The man was gone.

In that time of silence, I told the Lord I wanted the opportunity to speak to the man again and lay out the truth of how I felt about him. I repented because I had known years before that he was not someone God intended for me to be in a deep relationship with. Putting us in that position, though, had created a spiritual soul-tie or bond together that needed to be broken off, so that we could each be whole again. We had been Christians who were not careful with the other's heart. The Lord made these things clear to me.

It so happened that no reply came, but I had made another friend who went to a mutual event where this man was going to be, based on his patterns. I let her know what was going on, and she was glad to give me a ride. She was going to be leaving early, though, so she said I would have to find a ride home. The man I liked ended up being glad to give me a ride (and I had asked God for a small time to talk with the man but also for an opportunity to pay him back for all of the transportation when I didn't have a car). God answered my prayers because the man needed to fill his gas tank. This also let us have a few minutes to be 100% honest with each other about how we had been treating each other's hearts. His friend sat in the car, innocently waiting for us to finish filling the gas tank.

That felt like a joyfully infused breakup if ever I was to have one. After that night we became distant from each other but cordial in person. We did not harbor hard or bitter feelings toward each other, but we just did not feel a need to be together or to talk constantly. The soul-tie had been broken.

After that night I went into a time of feeling isolated. I had no friends; my family was far away, I was in low-income housing surrounded by women who were devoid of life, broken, depressed, mentally tortured, and not trustworthy. I felt some of the things they were dealing with and tried to help them, but I also felt loneliness and much stress from school and work. I gradually slipped into not writing and not opening up to people. I built walls for my self-protection.

In 2016 there was a different Christian man for whom I applied my newfound need for boundaries in opposite sex friendship. We became friends and enjoyed time together, like brother and sister, mostly during the day with others around. Occasionally, we spent time with each other alone, and in those times, again I opened up bit by bit. He seemed to like me and invited me to personal things. I felt again like perhaps this was someone that would be a good husband, but I was frustrated because he was not bold and did not like to lead or lacked confidence with leading. After a year of friendship he said that "he wasn't attracted to me, but he liked me, and maybe we could date after I finished college." I told him no and why, as gently as I could. It was another disappointment to my heart.

The only way anyone could know about the walls growing around my heart was if God had shown them or if they knew that I was not writing. It was a gradual process of shriveling up inside, but I saw my heart in December 2017 was like a raisin, dried out by weather and sun. I didn't know how to go to the Lord for a new life. But He is so good!

The SAME conference was in Kansas City. I begged God to use anyone to prophesy a word from Him over me. I wasn't hearing Him for myself. He did. The older woman said, "You are cherished by God. He said you have put walls up around your heart and create answers of defense in your mind before anyone speaks. He said you can trust Him. He loves you, and He will not throw you against a wall and hurt you." That was the start of new life flowing into my constrained and broken heart.

Since those heartbreaks and others, I re-learned that Jesus can handle my being vulnerable, and He won't ever push me away for being imperfect or living up to the high expectations I have for myself. He heals every hurt, pain, and loneliness I bring to Him.

In 2019 I finally became content with the idea of not relying on my own actions to "find a husband." When I learned Proverbs 18:22 (NLT) says, "The man who finds a wife, finds a treasure and receives favor from the Lord," I had much joy and peace. It removed pressure from myself trying to get any attention from men. Instead I could be my sometimes awkward, humorous, intelligent, creative self, knowing that Jesus' love for me is my completion. I actually did not believe anymore that someone else is my "other half" or that God would be so cruel as to break His own promise to my fifteen-year-old self about marriage. Instead I let those things be healed, and I pressed forward with the things and ministries I had before me, with nursing, ELI church, and hosting prayer meetings.

To my deepest surprise in 2020, among many other things that year contained, one of them was my fiancé! This man had been my friend whom I had held at what I considered arm's length for over a year. What happened is that I had thought "this guy will never be my husband because…," and I made a long, greatly detailed list for myself and others as to why he just wouldn't be my boyfriend or husband. What happened, in summary, is that I had an image and expectations of who the "perfectly matching man for me" would be, but God corrected that. Two weeks before March 5, 2020 (when we started dating), I was telling a girlfriend that "NO, I DO NOT like this guy. I will never be with him." It took God convicting my heart, showing me that I was looking through my own eyes of expectations, religious judgment, and pride, for me to reconsider my refusal. It took my acknowledging that I would not be trusting Jesus if I stuck with my own expectations and list.

March 5, 2020 I gave this man a chance to actually talk about our life perspectives and life trajectories. I found that what I considered "red flags" were actually misunderstandings and judgments that I held but had not taken the time to clarify. Because of a drive to Chicago, sharing a banana split at an antiquated diner, playing at a game lounge, and those things becoming our first date, I have learned so much more about being a real Christian. I have learned throughout 2020 that not even another person who is most intimate with you satisfies loneliness or depression, but they can help represent Christ. They can encourage, love, surprise, and support you in many ways. They also bring hurt from their lives and can bring out the hurts in your own life. With all of these hurts and feelings, I am learning that Jesus is still the greatest choice for bringing healing, because He heals them from the inside and replaces them with peace and healing from the inside out.

By the way, some of the things I wanted in my future husband, my fiance does have:

- Thoughtfulness

- Creativity

- Best hugs!!

- Biggest heart for God

- Generosity

- Love of children and desire to father orphans and foster children

Jesus is so faithful to our deepest desires that He gives to us! We might have fifteen-year-old selves with hundreds of our own made expectations, but those bring hurt. Jesus brings healing and the best surprises and adventures!

Psalm 37:4 "Delight yourself in the Lord and He will give you the desires of your heart."

Lindsey Schuler

Lindsey is a nurse residing in the United States of America. Pastimes include reading, walking, exploring, being part of ELI church, and spending quality time with family and her fiancé. Christian Writers Collective appealed to her because she loves Jesus and knows that He loves you too. She says, "There is none like Him, and I want to share: It is possible to have a living relationship with Him!"

19

† *There Are No Coincidences With God*

▼

by Karen Cousins

In my Christian walk, I believed in God, but my issue was believing in Jesus. I went to church until my early 20s, and when my brother and sisters were baptized, I could not bring myself to do it. I couldn't be baptized in the name of Jesus, when I wasn't sure I believed in Him.

I worked for a company that had four women (Kathye, Frankie, Carolyn, and Anna) who loved God and believed everything was possible through Jesus Christ. I questioned them. They had no shame in answering any questions or concerns. I visited their churches. God placed me in that office because He knew I needed work. I am a literal person and some of the stories in the Bible I found a little far-fetched. I also found the stories to be repetitive.

One day a pastor came into our office where I worked the front desk. He said, "You haven't been baptized." I wondered how on earth did he know that, and he offered to baptize me. I turned him down.

One day, I was visiting Roy (Kathye's husband) at the Music Parlor. He was talking to a guy outside. He said, "Whoa, wait a minute. You got a story to tell in the name of Jesus. I can't wait to hear it." I had no clue what he was talking about. WHAT STORY? His name was Dallas. His back story is that he used to be an alcoholic/drug addict. He told me how he was saved from his life of sin. I thought his story was amazing.

I changed jobs four years later and thought I was going to lose that connection and the insight I was gaining from these ladies. However, at my new job, there were three more ladies that walked that walk in the light of Jesus. I could talk to them about my walk. The three ladies (Kim, Pearline, and Roz) at the new job were absolute prayer warriors.

I thought I was smited by God. I called it, "my tears of a clown phase." I appeared to be happy, but I was dying inside. No one knew my real struggle. I told my friend that I didn't feel like I was praying right, because God turned His back on me. She told me as long as I was praying, He was listening. She said, "God wants to be your friend and wants to have an intimate relationship with you." I took that to heart, and I spoke out loud to Him everyday.

Roz told me that her brother had beaten alcoholism, drug abuse, and womanizing. He turned his life over to Christ. He asked Jesus for everything and was thankful that he could turn to the Lord. Her brother was a walking testimony to the name of Jesus. I was shocked to learn Roz's brother was Dallas. Yes, the same guy that told me that I had a story to tell. Now, how odd is that? God keeps working His magic.

That Sunday, I was watching *Sunday Best*. Alabaster Box was singing, and tears were streaming down my face. The words were just so powerful. I smelled the rain that night. I know God wanted me to have an understanding of His Son.

The next morning, I went to work, and Kathye had changed

jobs and had business in our office. She informed me that Roy opened a church, Oasis Word Ministries, in the Music Parlor. God doesn't make mistakes. He placed all of those ladies in my path for a reason. When I went to her church, on the wall was "I am...," which I thought was the shortest verse in the Bible, but it is not. I knew a powerful change was coming, because I thought, "I am..." says it all. It is powerful.

Genesis is my favorite book in the Bible. It is where it all begins. The first night, I went to the church, they prayed over me, and I felt it to the bone and smelled the rain. Roy told me bluntly that I wasn't God, and it wasn't for me to question the Word or understand everything in the Bible. He explained that God understands it, and He gave His only Son to save my soul. He had me read John 14:17.

It amazes me how God puts people in place for us to seek Him. In August of 2007 at the age of 36, I was baptized in the name of Jesus, and I believe. My life has been full with Jesus.

Note: Ms. Cousins has requested that no photo or bio of her be published in this book.

20

♡ *If You Let Him,*
Jesus Will Make You Whole

▼

by Michelle Jackson

Now that I had walked away and had died to my old life, I needed to know how to live. The questions were: live for what and live how? In my mind, I did not have any good reason to live, at least not any good enough for me to overcome all the hurts. It just seemed far more desirable and easier to die. I had put everything into this marriage. Now, I wanted no more pain and no more striving to achieve what seemed to be unattainable. I just wanted to give up.

There are many ways to die. The ones I thought most about were not physical, but they were more mental and spiritual. You see, I even wanted to do this easily. I wanted to just slip away and pretend I was really trying to live my best. Perhaps I could drown in alcohol, drugs, or maybe in depression. I contemplated all those things. However, being very afraid of drowning in any way, physical or spiritual or emotional, I could not do it. I needed a foundation of something to hold onto for purpose.

This is when my thoughts gravitated toward revenge. Now, that's something comfortable to hold onto for anyone in my present state. I had narrowly escaped committing property damage and even perhaps bodily harm, after finding my husband two-timing me. (If you read my testimony in the first *Jesus Can* ... volume, you know that my first instinct was to send a brick through his windshield. You also know that I did drop the brick.) I really should have felt relieved and much more thankful about that. Deep in my heart I did, but up top I still wanted revenge. No honestly, it was the reverse...more like deep in my heart I wanted revenge and up top I was thankful. My thankfulness was very shallow.

Because I was hurting, I wanted him to hurt too. Now, the

question was how to do that? Do I kill his dog? The death of his last dog was not my fault. Roscoe, his pitbull, was tied up in the backyard after getting loose numerous times and roaming the neighborhood. The police had already given us a warning, promising to ticket us the next time. Roy had tied Roscoe up himself. I did not touch him. I had no idea what was happening. It was a Saturday, and I was cooking and doing housework. Later that afternoon, when Roy got home from running errands, he found Roscoe dead. The dog had attempted to escape by jumping over the fence but instead got tangled up in the chain. Tragically, he ended up being strangled by the chain. Roy blamed me for not checking on him. I had no idea what he was talking about as I had nothing to do with the dog because I did not like pitbulls.

As I contemplated revenge, my thoughts just could not get into any sinister actions, such as physically hurting people or even animals. Now, if I am upset, I do not mind hurting feelings when I think it is well deserved. In this case, Roy's feelings getting hurt were, in my opinion, more than well deserved.

Like most women when trying to get back at an ex, I looked for a new relationship. I wanted to hurt Roy. Besides, the way to get over an old relationship is to become involved in a new one. At least, this was the advice I was given from the world.

While silently planning to lose weight, look better, and get a new boyfriend, I kept up my commitment to reading the Bible daily. I had not liked the image of myself reflected in Roy's windshield when I was about to break it. This is what led me to try to get help. In my readings, I discovered that Christ wants to give me that help. He wants a relationship too. He promises things like love and acceptance, as well as faithfulness, meaning He will never leave me. I had accepted Him as my Lord and Savior, believing in Him to do what He said He would do.

Just like when I got into a relationship with Roy, I did not know what to expect getting into a relationship with Christ. This time, though, I was much better off than the last time. He had been right here with me all the time, but I had rejected and ignored Him. Don't we all, women and men alike, tend to ignore the best person for us?

As I read more about Jesus and got to know Him better, my desire to be with Him and talk to Him grew too. His attention to my needs were staggering to me. I was not sure what

He wanted from me, so I asked Him. He said that He wanted to make me whole. I thought I was fine and told Him so. He could see right through me. However, right then the thoughts of revenge came to my mind. He said again, I want to make you whole. I immediately started to cry. Then I realized that in all that had happened, I had never before cried. Deep heartfelt cries began to come out of me. I had wanted to hold onto it, but now it was all coming out of me. Like the ugliness that revenge and unforgiveness really are, they began to spill out of me. A part of me wanted to hold onto them, but His words were just too powerful for me to resist.

I realized my sin was idolizing marriage and Roy himself. I had looked to this marriage solely for companionship, protection, and enjoyment. You see, I was running away from a home without any of those things. There's nothing wrong with these things in and of themselves, but they are only benefits and blessings that God provides within the confines of marriage.

Ironically, I was behaving just like a man wanting the benefits without the commitment. This commitment was to God. The point was that I was not in this marriage to glorify God but only to bless myself. These were legitimate needs. Being scared of being on my own, however, I'd tried to satisfy those needs through another human being rather than by turning to God. No matter what my motive, it still did not make it right.

I was not trying to develop a Christlike character to show a picture of Christ's relationship to the church either. At that time, I didn't even understand what that meant or know that this was God's purpose for marriage. Unfortunately, my ignorance does not change the fact that I was sinning. I would have perhaps known this if I was in a personal relationship with Jesus. In this relationship I would have known at least that I could depend on Him. Now that I know these things, everything has changed.

Most pertinent to the theme of this volume, being in a relationship with Christ has healed many of my past hurts. I must admit that I am still working on some, but at least I am now headed in the right direction. His love and acceptance have shown me my own sin. This in turn has helped me to forgive others—even a two-timing husband. I now know what to live for and how to live. I'm to glorify Him and tell others about Him. Some of you know Him and some do not.

For those who do not, I sincerely hope that you won't miss out on having a personal relationship with Him. He really can heal your hurts if you allow Him. He can truly make you whole.

Michelle Jackson

Michelle Jackson is a Chicago native who has lived in Milwaukee since 2008. By day, she works as an energy-industry analyst. But her lifelong dream is to write fiction and non-fiction, exploring through storytelling the parallel existence of physical and spiritual laws. Her debut work, *A Prisoner's Pardon*, delves deep into the issue of prison reform as an answer to recidivism, and the Word of God as the truth that can set anyone free.

21

† *Always by Me*

▼

---

by Dr. John Click

My mother told me that as a baby I was very sick. In fact, I was not expected to live when I was five weeks old. The local doctors were perplexed and had given up on helping me. The prognosis was not good. The only thing left to do was to transfer me to a local Children's Hospital in hopes of getting answers. My mother fervently prayed for me this entire time. I went to the new hospital and was kept in Intensive Care. After two weeks there, a retired pediatrician finally was able to diagnose my problem. My mother's prayers were answered, and I was miraculously sent home. It was a blessing that the retired doctor was in the right place at the right time to help me. One might say God placed her there.

As a child I was raised in a southern Baptist home. Our lives were filled with the family going to Sunday School, Sunday church services, as well as church again on some Sunday nights and Wednesdays. In the summer we naturally attended Vacation Bible school (VBS). You've got to love those VBS cookies and kool-aid! We kids did. I had friends in church, and it was just a regular part of my life for many years.

I accepted Jesus as my Savior when I was twelve years old. We had confirmation classes, and my confession of faith was the next step. I didn't really feel different, but I knew I had accepted Jesus as my Savior. Nothing really changed, but I kept going to church. Church was a tremendous part of my life growing up until about the age of thirteen. Like every other teenager I felt the need to make some spending money. Not many people would hire a thirteen year old, but I landed a job that regrettably required me to work on Sundays. Looking back, I wish my mom would have just said no, because church was first. My job unfortunately led to about nine years of no real church involvement. Through junior high school, high school, and college, I missed going to church. Once that habit is broken, it is hard to start it again. There were a lot of bad influences and worldly activities in my life that replaced church, and most of all, some really bad choices. I needed church and God but did not realize it.

Despite myself, God had something else in store for me besides failure or harm. He had good plans for me. I did work very hard in college and was counseled to apply for dental school. The results of my exam revealed that I scored well enough to be accepted. This was another blessing from God. Once I entered dental school, it didn't take very long to realize that I needed to have God back in my life if I was going to be successful.

Even though I was twelve when I was baptized, I really didn't understand the scope of Jesus' love for me until I was age twenty-three. I was extremely depressed and away from home. My classwork was hard. I felt alone, like I was going to be a failure, and that no one cared. It was very cold in Indianapolis that night, and I decided to walk out onto a frozen lake. My hope was that perhaps I would fall through the ice. That, however, was not God's plan for me. As I began walking on that thin ice, I felt a physical pull drawing me back to Christ in that very moment. He was calling me back to Him. Through tears I made the decision to turn back to Jesus rather than keep going on my dangerous journey to the center of the lake. Jesus was there patiently waiting for me to come back. I felt Him guiding me as I slipped off of the frozen water onto the safe land. He was there with me. I knew He had led me off of that lake. For the first time in years, I had an assurance that He was directing and supporting me. I knew it would never end, and He would continue to be with me throughout my life.

I know now, it was God that kept me focused even when I went through stages of depression due to the grueling course load. He held me in His arms and never let me go. I was a ship without a rudder in a windstorm, but God was there in my darkest moments. He captained my life and welcomed me with open, loving arms.

I became involved in a dental school Bible study and started to attend church regularly. Things started positively changing for me then. I met a wonderful Christian woman, who was my rock in every storm. God put her in my path to help me get closer to Him. My walk with God became stronger and stronger.

God placed me in a rural community that drastically needed a dentist. I have also needed them just as much. This has become a mission field for me. Thirty-five years later my story just keeps going. God has constantly provided for me in every way, shape, and form. Learning to trust in Him has been my life's greatest lesson. God never walks away. I cannot imagine the prayers that my wife and mother have poured out before God. He heard every one of them. Fourteen years ago I had a surgery mishap, and I was ready to meet my Lord and Savior. That was not His plan. God was not ready for me. With the help of many Christian brothers and sisters, I was able to recover and even maintain my practice.

I am so very blessed that God has been with me every step of my life. I have fallen and needed to be picked up several times. Our God is a forgiving Father. He has always been there. He has held me in victory and defeat. God has comforted me and has humbled me. Believe me, I have needed a good dose of humility several times. He has welcomed me as a loving Father would. I truly praise God that He gave me a mother who believed in Him and knew the importance of raising her children to develop a relationship with Him, also. Praise God for all He has done and will continue to do!

Proverbs 22:6

John Patrick Click, DDS

John Patrick Click, DDS, is a practicing dentist in Southern Indiana. He and wife, Sharon, have been married over thirty years and have three grown children. Dr. Click is an Adjunct Professor of Anatomy, United States Naval Veteran, musician, and Christian.

22

 There's Always a Purpose

by Nichole Tenny

I didn't always know what my purpose was, being raised in a dysfunctional family. Having an abusive father that dealt drugs and a mother who eventually became an addict, I thought my purpose was to survive. Just making it through the day sometimes was a victory for me. My mother eventually left my father. Then she, my brother, and I went to live with my grandmother. We lived in fear that he would come back and hurt us. I was afraid of the dark, my stomach was often in knots; I felt frightened and alone. I remember going through some dark times and thinking there had to be a reason.

I was raised Catholic. I went to church with my grandmother every Sunday. She was the only constant stability in my life.

In first grade, developmental issues were discovered, and I had to repeat the year and go to another school with a classroom full of children in wheelchairs who couldn't speak. Praise God for the teacher who recognized and informed my mother and grandmother that I did not belong in that class. My grandmother took me to St. Patrick's school, where they worked with my learning disability.

When my mother remarried, she and I moved in with her new husband. This is when my life would be altered forever. I remember my room, the place I hid from the stress and tension, anger, and fear. I remember the first time he came into my room, the smell of alcohol, and him climbing on me and telling me he knew what was best for me and what I needed. If I was quiet he wouldn't hurt me. He would restrain me, and he introduced me to pornography. I remember thinking, where was God? How could He let me go through this? Oh how I wished I could go back to the safety of being with my grandmother and brother.

The abuse I suffered was not just sexual, but also emotional and physical. This sadistic torment went on for 3 1/2 years. I became withdrawn and detached. Once the traumatic abuse stopped, I began to self abuse. In my young mind, I thought that burning myself with erasers would erase what had happened. I also started cutting, trying to cut the pain out. Cutting became my go-to thing. Once I got numb to that, I started looking at the very thing he used to trap me, pornography. I hated it, so why did I struggle with it for so long?

This is right where my story could have ended, seemingly broken at fourteen years old. High school was tough, but I made it to graduation. That was a day that I thought would never happen. Then it was time to decide what to do with my life. A hairstylist was what I wanted to be. After working for a year on my first job, I gave my heart to Jesus, and my life has never been the same. Soon after that, I started Bible college. Before I knew it, I graduated from college with a Bachelor's Degree! After acceptance into the Master's program for counseling, I thought back to first grade and how far I'd come. Also, through all the darkness was a realization of God's constant presence.

People have tried to put labels of learning disability, broken, neglected, victim, and dysfunctional on me. I allowed the world to label me for my entire life. I'm grateful to say now that I don't live that way anymore. Forgiveness is the key to my continual journey of freedom. Also, knowing that when you totally surrender to Jesus and partner with Him, He can give your pain a purpose.

I believe that your name says a lot about you. Have you ever looked up what your name means? Nichole means "victory of the people, overcomer." That's who I am in Jesus. I don't believe in coincidences. God had a purpose all along.

I found my purpose, which is coming alongside people to give hope and encouragement, bring courage and strength to those who are weary, and be the agent of change for my family and friends and all with whom I come in contact. The Bible promises us that in this world we will have trouble, but we are to take heart, because Jesus has overcome the world for us.

Nichole Tenny

My name is Nichole Tenny. I am a hairstylist and I use my work as a platform to minister to people. I am fun-loving, lighthearted, and prefer a comedic approach to life. My passion for mental and spiritual health prompted my bachelor's degree in community ministry. I'm now pursuing my master's degree in counseling. My hope is that God continues to use my life to inspire and encourage others.

23

✝ *Unconditional Love*

▼

by Cheri Swalwell

I consider myself blessed. There isn't a time in my life when I can't remember hearing the name Jesus spoken with love in my household. My parents both came from Christian homes as well, and there is a long line of ministry-related occupations in my lineage—ministers, traveling evangelists, Christian radio show hosts, speakers, writers and musicians.

I clearly remember giving my life to Jesus at the age of six. It was a rainy Saturday afternoon, and I was washing the dishes with my older sister, my mom listening in as she worked alongside us. Once again, my mouth got me in trouble. I was feisty back then and still have to reign that aspect of my life in, at times today. My mom took me to my room and began talking to me about how mean I was being, talking badly about one of our friends. I don't remember the full conversation or even what I had been saying about our friend, but I do remember feeling the Holy Spirit's conviction and wanting to ask Jesus into my heart that day. I prayed the sinner's prayer with my mom by my bedside.

God knew that when I prayed that prayer as a six year old that my name was forever written in His Book of Life; however, I had a lot of faith-growing to do before I reached the same level of confidence. Even though my father, who was also my pastor, taught grace from the pulpit, I grew up in the "Don't get left behind" era where End-Time movies were shown often in youth group or Sunday evening services. Every time there was a movie like that, I would rededicate my life to God, not completely understanding the true meaning of faith and grace, fearful the prayer hadn't stuck the first, fifth, or tenth time. Even as an adult, after having moved away from my parents' church, I had misguided pastors in my life. A few questioned my salvation, further causing me to doubt what I knew deep down had taken place beside my bed that rainy Saturday afternoon. I was a child of God and nothing could separate me from His love.

I'm not sure where, or when, I started believing the concept of God as a judge, sitting up in heaven, simply waiting for me to mess up so He could punish me. I lived in fear of the One I was supposed to trust. I avoided Him when I sinned and couldn't comprehend calling Him "Abba, Daddy."

However, Abba knew my heart and how I had willingly given it to Him back when I was six years old. He, in all His loving kindness, wasn't satisfied with a polite relationship with me. He wanted all of me, and He wanted me to experience all of Him. The real Him.

I have always heard how children, especially those who have accepted Jesus into their hearts at a young age, have to make their relationship with God their own. It's great growing up hearing the stories of how God shows up in your parents' lives, but it's life-changing when you see Him show up and work miracles in your own.

I didn't understand what that meant until Abba met my simple request with His unconditional, over-the-top love.

"I don't think I trust, You, God, but I want to. Help me learn how to trust You, but please be gentle."

The next six years God ceased being that stern, fearsome judge high in the sky waiting to punish me the second I sinned, and instead became the daddy I couldn't wait to crawl up into His lap and ask for help. Sometimes He would tell me no to my requests, sometimes it was wait, and sometimes He would answer yes. I learned how to trust that each of His responses was for my own good, that He truly wanted the best for my life, even more than I did. I learned that my spiritual maturity was more important to Him than a temporary fix. I learned that I could trust Him with my jobs, my paycheck, and most importantly, the safety and health of my family. I learned that He truly does love to give good gifts to His children, and sometimes those good gifts are wrapped in hardship, but as long as He is right there with me, I can face anything, trusting that He has a plan that is for my good.

What are some of the miracles that He brought into my life? First, He worked on building my faith and removing fear itself from my life. Then, He removed my decade-plus fear of winter driving. He also miraculously healed me from depression, then seasonal depression, and taught me how to gain victory over panic attacks. He allowed me to experience His peace "that passes all understanding" to the point where I don't want to live without it present in my life.

I have learned how to hear His voice, and He has begun speaking to me in so many different ways—through colors while I'm praying, through my dreams, through that still, small voice, through Scripture, through mentors, and audibly while praying with my prayer partner.

Of all the things God has taught me, do you know what my favorite thing is besides the fact I know I can completely trust Him? Life is an adventure with God, and as long as I am staying close to His side, it's more amazing than I could have ever dreamed possible.

Cheri Swalwell

Cheri Swalwell is a Christ follower, wife, mother, writer, and speaker, in that order. You'll find Cheri encouraging others through her fiction and nonfiction books (www.cheriswalwell.com) or weekly on Cheer UP Podcast with host and friend, Kara Hunt. Whenever possible, she loves spending time outdoors with her husband, three kids, and two dogs.

24

♡ *Jesus Answers My Desperate Prayer*

by James Koenig

The death of a loved one is an exceptionally difficult experience to bear. As a Christian, it is even harder if the deceased is unsaved, having never made Jesus their Lord and Savior. When my older sister, Mary Kay, died in 2016, my heart was heavy with uncertainty and sorrow, for I did not know if she had made a life-changing decision for Christ.

Death is inevitable, but when it comes, we are rarely prepared. My loving mother, Marian, died suddenly in 1999 of an undiagnosed aortic aneurysm. When it burst, my mother collapsed and passed into heaven instantly. The last face she saw was my sister, Debbie, who witnessed her fall to the ground and pass away. Mom was the heart and soul of our family. Losing her so suddenly, without a chance to say "goodbye" was heart-wrenching for all of us. I was forty-five years old, and I cried as I have never cried before.

After weeks of mourning for her, I turned to the scriptures for comfort. In John 14:3, Jesus tells His disciples, "And if I go and prepare a place for you, I will come again and will take you to myself, that where I am you may be also." My mom was a faithful Christian who believed in the divinity of Jesus. Since this verse promised that mom was with the Lord, I pictured my mom in heaven, happily reunited with her mother, father, and brothers, and my sorrow lifted. Realizing my mom was beginning a new eternal life in heaven was transforming for me. While I missed my mom terribly, I was happy for her. She had received her promised reward for being a faithful follower of Christ Jesus.

Mary Kay, my older sister by two years, loved my mom with all her heart. And while she knew Mom was in heaven, Mary

Kay was not a professed Christian believer. Mary Kay had an extremely difficult relationship with our father, who was a harsh and cold man. I believe this crucial and developmentally failed relationship led her to the belief that she could not trust men, and ultimately, she also could not relate to or trust a father in heaven. My conversion to Christianity became a dividing point between Mary Kay and myself. We had numerous unproductive discussions about the Bible, both of us ending up frustrated and angry with each other. Mary Kay was not an atheist but believed in the "many pathways to heaven" concept. For her, all religions were essentially equal, and what truly mattered was whether one was a "good" person or not. She believed Christianity was a misogynistic, male-dominated hierarchy that belittled women as second-class citizens.

Growing up, Mary Kay was somewhat of a rebel. She had difficulties in school and at home, and she was a source of frequent consternation to my mother and father. Mary Kay began smoking at age fifteen, sneaking cigarettes from my dad's cigarette pack. This began a lifetime habit of smoking that ended up in a diagnosis of emphysema at age forty-five. Since emphysema is a slowly progressive illness, Mary Kay's lung capacity decreased each year. When she entered her sixties, she began to use supplemental oxygen. By the age of 63, Mary Kay needed oxygen twenty-four hours a day and was facing her impending death. Her doctor advised her to consider a lung transplant, and Mary Kay entered a long waiting list of people who needed a transplant to continue their lives.

The call for the transplant came in September 2016. Mary Kay called me the morning she got the call and told me she was headed to the hospital at that moment to undergo the lung transplant procedure. I immediately said a prayer for her and told her I would visit her as soon as she came out of surgery.

Lung transplantation is a difficult surgery and requires a long recovery period. The most feared complication is infection, specifically pneumonia in the new lung. And within a week of the procedure, Mary Kay's new lung had pneumonia. She became gravely ill and lapsed into a coma. As her organs began to fail due to a lack of oxygen, her blood ammonia level began to climb to a dangerously toxic level. Her doctors put her on a blood dialysis machine 24/7 in an attempt to save her life. For three long weeks, Mary Kay remained in a coma, hanging on to life by a slim thread. My two other sisters and I prayed for her constantly. I was also burdened by the knowledge that Mary Kay was not saved. She had never accepted Jesus as her Savior.

And then our prayers were answered. The ammonia levels began to drop and then became normal. We did not know if the elevated ammonia had damaged her body and brain, which was certainly a real possibility. About a week later, Mary Kay opened her eyes and came back to us. Her body and mind had not been damaged by the near-lethal ammonia level. While Mary Kay could not talk to us due to a tracheal tube in her throat, she could express her mind through her eyes and by nodding or shaking her head. One night, after her other visitors had left, I took her hand and said a prayer for the salvation of her soul. I asked Mary Kay to hear my prayer and accept the Lord Jesus as her Savior. I told the Lord that she had been critically damaged by her dysfunctional relationship with our father. I asked the Lord to forgive her for her inability or unwillingness to seek a relationship with Jesus. I prayed about Jesus's sacrifice on the cross. I told Mary Kay that Mom was in heaven and that if she wanted to see Mom again, she needed to confess her sins and make the Lord her Savior. During the prayer, Mary Kay kept her eyes open and stared at me the entire time. Since she could not talk, I did not know her response to the prayer.

About a week later, I visited her on a Sunday evening. She had recovered a bit more and the nurses had helped her into a chair. She was watching television. She still had the breathing tube in her throat so she could not speak. She appeared profoundly depressed, with unexpressive dead eyes. I asked her if she had accepted the prayer of salvation that we had prayed together, and she just stared at me. I asked her to nod or shake her head to answer, but she only stared at me, giving no indication as to her state of mind. Apparently, she was still undecided. Before I left, I knelt down, gently took her hand, and told her that none of us have any guarantee about tomorrow and that her situation was even more critical. I asked her again to surrender her life and future to Jesus.

Five days later, on a Friday morning, I received a call at work from my sister, Debbie, telling me that Mary Kay had died that morning of sudden cardiac arrest. I met Debbie at Mary Kay's hospital room. We mourned for her as we sat by her now dead body. When it was time to leave, I kissed her on the forehead and said a final prayer that she had accepted Jesus as her Savior.

Her funeral came and went, and I had no satisfaction in regards to her salvation. I did not know if she had reunited with our mom in heaven. It was a question that deeply troubled me, for I did not want to imagine the awful alternative.

Several weeks later, I desperately prayed to the Lord to tell me in some way, by some sign, if Mary Kay was saved and in heaven. About a month later, the answer to my prayer came in the form of a vivid "divine" dream. Up to that point in my life, I had experienced three other divine dreams as I call them, so I knew this dream was special. Divine dreams are different from regular dreams. My divine dreams are always in vivid color, make perfect logical sense, have a definite purpose or message, and I also remember every single detail of the dream upon awakening. In this divine dream, I was sitting on my parent's couch with my two other sisters. Suddenly, Mary Kay walked into the room and sat down across from us in my mom's favorite chair. Of all the chairs in the room, she sat in my mother's chair. She calmly crossed her legs and looked at us. When she suffered from chronic emphysema, Mary Kay had a pallid bluish-gray pallor to her skin and just did not look healthy. But now, Mary Kay looked exceptionally healthy and vibrant again. She was smartly dressed in dark slacks, a light blue blouse, and a black vest. She looked supremely happy. I immediately asked her if she had accepted the prayer of salvation I had prayed with her in the hospital. She looked at me and gave me the biggest smile I had ever seen. She nodded her head once and continued to beam that radiant smile. At that point the dream abruptly ended and I awoke. I knew this was the answer to my fervent prayer! I wept with thanksgiving and gratitude to the Lord for being so gracious in answering my prayer. By sitting in my mom's favorite chair, I knew this was symbolic of Mary Kay being reunited in heaven with our beloved mother. Mary Kay was now enjoying a new life in heaven. I was overjoyed and tears flowed from my eyes like a torrent. Jesus had answered my prayer in a miraculous way. He took the uncertainty and gloom I had in my heart and turned it into complete joy.

I don't know why the Lord blessed me with this dream. I have prayed just as fervently for other issues and other people and never received a direct answer. Perhaps the answers to those prayers are in the future, or I will find out in heaven. Whatever the case, I am so grateful that the Lord revealed to me Mary Kay's salvation. He took away my sorrow and gave me absolute joy.

If you don't know if you are saved, please realize that you can be certain if you are a saved child of God. Romans 10:9

states, "If you confess with your mouth, 'Jesus is Lord,' and believe in your heart that God raised Him from the dead, you will be saved." If you have unsaved loved ones, please present the gospel message to them in a kind and gentle way. We don't know when our last breath or heartbeat will be, nor do we know how much time our loved ones have. Be bold. You may be the person through whom the gospel message is presented. Your testimony may be the seed that blooms into eternal life.

I don't know if I was used by the Lord in presenting the gospel to Mary Kay, or if she would have surrendered her heart to Jesus before she died. I do know this: Mary Kay survived a difficult lung transplant surgery (a small miracle in itself), survived almost certain death from pneumonia and elevated ammonia level (a much larger miracle), and then lived long enough thereafter to accept the Lord as her Savior (another tremendous miracle)! I'm thankful if my prayer was the impetus that changed her life and led her to eternal life with Jesus. I'm even more thankful that she has reunited with our mother in heaven, and that she now is experiencing the love of Jesus. And I'm happy that someday I will reunite with my mother, father, and Mary Kay in heaven. Yes, my father became a Christian late in his life, and that is yet another miraculous story I am eternally grateful to have witnessed.

Jesus can heal our hurts. He only asks that we trust in Him and follow Him. I'm so glad that I did, and I know that my mom, dad, and Mary Kay would say the same.

James Koenig

Jim is sixty-five years old, has been married for thirty years, and is the father of six children. He is a dentist by profession but has a wide range of interests, including photography, Christian apologetics, reading, writing, fishing, hiking, and traveling. He lives in rural Forest Lake, Minnesota.

25

✝ *No Rain…No Rainbows*

▼

by Connie Hensley

Growing up in a small town in Kentucky, the only child of devoted loving parents, certainly not wealthy, but always having everything I needed and much of what I wanted, all was right with the world. I truly was blessed as a child to have both sets of grandparents very much involved in my up-bringing. I can still hear my grandmother singing "What a Friend We Have in Jesus," and I can see her sweet mischie-vous smile. We never had serious talks about heaven and hell, but her life was a true testimony of her faith. Always content,

Ma's joy came from deep inside, and somehow I knew it was coming from God because it certainly did not come from her circumstances.

She shared her life with me, and I'm convinced that she helped lead me to the One who could provide that same joy in my life. At the age of seven, while visiting a revival meeting with my cousin, I experienced something I had never before experienced. Fifty-nine years later, I can't tell you the title of the hymn or even any of the words, but I knew without a doubt that the Holy Spirit was speaking to my heart through the music. I returned home and told my parents what had happened and shared with them my desire to be baptized. That was the beginning of my Christian journey...and what a journey it has been!

My adult journey began by marrying my high school sweetheart at the age of twenty. Two years later our first son was born, but sadly, our marriage was already in trouble. Twenty-three months passed, and our second son joined our turbulent family. Two years later I was a single mom with two little boys. This was not the Norman Rockwell image of life that I had grown up with! Although in those college years, being involved in church was not a priority in my life, I always knew God was with me. His faithfulness is flawless…mine is not.

The next step in the journey was a second marriage that brought with it some real eye-opening events. You see this godly man had lost his first wife to cancer, and they were both dear friends of mine. Because he was a preacher and I was divorced, some in the church did not approve of our marriage. Some believed that my divorce was the main issue, while others thought our marriage was too soon. I was devastated and left feeling like a dirty, useless, marked woman. As I look back, I can better understand those negative reactions and can see how God used this to help me be more understanding of other people.

This marriage is now forty years old and has taken us down a few roads that no one would enjoy, but because we are both devoted to God and to each other, we have weathered these storms together. God and God alone could have provided the strength we've needed to survive major depression, huge financial battles, a thirty-year battle involving one son and drugs, and the devastating news of brain cancer in another. I tell you all this to say, God is faithful. He provides one day at a time. There is rain in every life, but it's the rain along with the "Sonshine" that produces those beautiful rainbows that remind us of God's everlasting promises. Remember, "No rain, no rainbows." Just as that beautiful rainbow stretches across the sky, so have the troubles of this world stretched me and caused me to dig deep into the Truth of God's Word. That's where He became "My God," not the God of my parents and grandparents, but MY personal, always with me, loving God.

God is faithful in all situations, and we can grow in relationship with Him through each step of life. His word is Truth, and He commands us in Joshua 1:9 to be "strong and courageous, do not be afraid and do not be discouraged for the Lord your God will be with you wherever you go." I can testify to His faithfulness!!!

Connie Hensley

Connie is blessed to be a daughter, wife, mother, mother-in-love, grandmother, and friend to some wonderful people. She is retired from her local Telecommunications Company where she spent most of her career as the Purchasing Agent. The past forty years she's been "the preacher's wife," serving congregations in Kentucky and South Carolina. Teaching, leading Bible studies, directing children's musicals, and occasionally doing speaking engagements have been areas of service for many years.

The joy of her life is serving God and loving her family and friends. Cooking, crafting, writing poetry, and party planning are hobbies that Connie enjoys. She and her husband, Wayne, call south central Kentucky home.

26

♡ *Jesus Can Heal Financial and Emotional Hurts*

by Robert Thibodeau

When I was in the Army, I was 100% committed to my career. When that career was suddenly and unexpectedly over, I was lost. I felt like I had no purpose in life. My life lost its meaning.

My health suffered (I gained almost fifty pounds in one year). I started drinking heavily. Financially I struggled. I was angry all the time. (And I have to admit—I was "lost" spiritually as well). My life was a mess.

Insurance sales helped to pay some of the bills. I was good at what I did. I always ranked in the top ten salesmen for our company, but the income was inconsistent. We did not know from one week to the next if there was any paycheck coming. Additionally, if there was a paycheck, we never knew the amount until we actually received it. Our bills kept getting farther and farther past due.

Then, the first Gulf War (Operation Desert Storm) started, and my market base (the military market) was shipped 6,000 miles across sea. Now, I had no income. This drove me deeper into my depression.

I decided to move myself to Columbus, Georgia. Fort Benning is a training facility, and they would have people there, even in wartime. I packed up and moved into a little dumpy, unfurnished apartment on January 1, 1992. Our bills were way, way late. I needed to make some money. I left my family back in Louisiana and decided this was the only option for me to try and make money. Twenty-five days later, I had sold zero. Nothing. Nada.

My wife called and said the electric company was going to turn off the lights. The mortgage was three months in arrears and ready to go into foreclosure. She had no money left in the house, and there was no food for the kids. What was she going to do? What was I going to do?

I hung up the phone and cried…I cried out in despair…

Then, it came to me. I would kill myself, and they could have the insurance money. I had my policy long enough so I knew the company would pay. My wife could use the proceeds to pay off the house, pay for college for the kids, and still be okay with what was left over to maintain her life. That was the plan.

The clock revealed that it was already 11:30 at night. I wanted to tell my kids that I loved them one more time. I decided that I would call them as they prepared for school in the morning—then that would be it.

Through a miraculous intervention that night—God told me everything would be all right. I had my grandfather's Bible with me. It was on the floor and as I lay there on the floor to go to sleep, I was at peace with my decision. I looked at the Bible again. It was illuminated by a street light from outside shining on it. I decided it might be a good idea to read the Bible, since I was going to meet God the next day. At least I could tell Him I had read the Bible…

In the front was a Bible Reading Plan. I looked up January

25th and the scripture for that day was Psalm 34. As I started to read, I got to verse 7 which said, "The Lord has heard this poor man cry and shall deliver him from all his troubles."

My spirit suddenly EXPLODED on the inside of me! I started laughing, crying, praying in tongues—all at one time! I knew I had just been born again. I carried on like that for at least ten or fifteen minutes. Then, I knew I had to call my wife. She had been born again four years earlier and had been praying for me. It was at her insistence that I took my grandfather's Bible with me to Georgia.

When I told her what happened, we both started rejoicing. I told her I would be home on January 31st (it was a month-to-month lease). Realistically, I could be just as broke at home with her and our kids as I could be by myself.

Well, between January 26th and January 31st, I sold enough insurance to pay my bills in Georgia and start to catch-up on the bills back home. I experienced supernatural intervention on so many levels.

Six months later, we moved to Killeen, Texas, and were able to buy a house there. I opened my own insurance agency and within just three years, we had the #2 producing agency in our company. What a blessing!

Within one year, I had completely quit drinking alcohol. The best part is that I never knew I quit until six months after I stopped drinking. God gets all of the glory there.

I had purchased a little pint bottle of whiskey in November 1992. Had one drink and just didn't like the taste that night. In May 1993, there was a leak under the kitchen sink. When I went to clean out that area so I could fix the pipe, there was that half bottle of whiskey. It was then I realized that I had not had one drink in six months. I have never had the taste for it since. Praise God!

Life has not been a constant bed of roses. We have had issues since then. I have never, ever doubted that Jesus can make things better. Even in the midst of chaos, I rest in the Lord. I have never doubted, even once, since that night, on January 25, 1992 that JESUS IS LORD!

I say all that just so you know—"Jesus CAN Heal Your Hurts!" No matter what they are!

Pastor Robert Thibodeau

Pastor Robert Thibodeau is a twelve-year Army veteran, serving as both enlisted and a commissioned Cavalry Officer. He is a retired law enforcement supervisor. After his retirement, he started his radio career. Within six months he accepted an opportunity to be on AM radio, nationwide. He is the founder of Podcasters for Christ and helps Christian podcasters, ministers, authors, and musicians, to share the Word through online media, including radio. Please visit https://podcastersforchrist.com for more information.

27

† *My Help Comes from the Lord of Miracles*

▼

by Deborah Quinones-Vázquez

I lift up my eyes to the mountains— where does my help come from? My help comes from the LORD, the Maker of Heaven and Earth.
Psalms 121:1, 2.

The sun was so bright and warm, yet for some reason I felt chills as I walked that morning into the doctor's office. I cannot remember if I was cold or just shaking with nerves.

Everything moved in slow motion, or so it seemed to me. I know there was noise and people also talking softly in the waiting room. I remember the TV was on as well. But all I could hear was my heart pounding fast inside my ears, and I kept repeating Psalm 121 over and over again.

I had been told by my ENT to get a PET/CT scan. He had explained the test and procedure to me, but I did not understand one word he said. My nerves by now had gotten the best of me. Again, the results had not been favorable.

I couldn't bring myself to say the word "cancer." I thought if I say it, it will become true. All I kept saying was ... "My help, trust, and confidence come from the Lord, the Maker of heaven and Earth."

Of course, on that May morning in 2011, nothing was all right. After speaking to my doctor, everything became a blur as if time had stood still. That same day after the PET/CT scan, he also ordered lab work and an ECG. He informed me that I would be having surgery on Tuesday to remove the cancer.

That night I went to bed and began to speak to God. I remember praying; "Though I walk through the valley of the shadow of death, I will fear no evil: for Thou art with me;

Thy rod and Thy staff they comfort me." Psalms 23:4. I fell asleep repeating it.

Two days later was Mother's Day, and my family had come together to have dinner at my brother's house. His wife's mother, who is now in heaven, told me, "As I prayed for you today in church, God spoke to my heart and said; "Tell Debbie that I have healed her." Immediately I felt peace come over me like a soft breeze on a warm summer day. I knew in my heart this was true.

The Tuesday morning of my surgery, I arrived at the hospital along with my family. I was a bit nervous, but I kept thinking that I was told I was healed. I kept repeating in my head, "My help comes from the Lord…"

I don't remember talking to the doctor that day. I knew I had not seen my family and twelve hours had already gone by when I noticed the time. I dozed on and off a few times. I was now awake, and I noticed I was in a regular room. I thought, "Okay, I never went into ICU, the way I was told to expect." That was good.

Later that evening the doctor's assistant spoke to me and my family. He told us I had lymph nodes removed, but they found no cancer, and that my doctor would speak to us the following day. I felt this immense joy come over me. Glory of God and a testimony to the Power in the mighty name of Jesus, I was healed.

God performed a miracle in my life. All traces of cancer were now gone. More than five tests could not be mistaken, I understood the power of prayer in the name of Jesus. It was a miracle! Glory to God.

As I slept in a regular hospital room that night, I kept repeating, "I lift up my eyes to the mountains— where does my help come from?" And I answered each time, "My help came from the LORD, the Maker of Heaven and Earth." Psalms 121:1, 2.

I could now understand what Job said, "My ears had heard of You; but now (in my deepest pain) my eyes had seen HIM!"

Deborah Quinones-Vázquez

Deborah Quinones-Vázquez is a translator and ordained minister who has helped victims of Hurricane Maria. She was recognized by the New York State Comptroller's Office of New York and Hispanic Heritage Association of Western New York for her dedication and compassion. Deborah began writing at sixteen and is currently working on a book of inspirational poems, prose, and a short personal story. Born in New York, she now resides in Georgia.

28

♡ *Perfected Peace at the End*

▼

by Wm. David Waterman

When my mother passed away, I learned the meaning of this scripture, 1 Thessalonians 4:13. It reads: "But I would not have you to be ignorant, brethren, concerning them which are asleep, that ye sorrow not, even as others which have no hope."

Mom was committed to church. We often laughed at the joke that is told in pulpits about how the person testifying had a "drug" problem because their parents drug them to church every time it was open. Such was the case for me and my siblings. We were drug to church every time it opened, and for every event my mother would arrange her schedule to attend.

Her faithfulness and seeking after God started out as religion in a denominational church and progressed to a relationship with God through Jesus Christ. Her attitude toward the great majority of people she encountered was one of graciousness and consideration for their situation. As a result, she often reached people that even pastors couldn't seem to reach. I watched as she treated people of all races equally and with the same grace. It made a huge impact on me, and I found that it had permeated my lifestyle as well.

I learned as I grew up that doors opened and opportunities came to people who walked as Jesus walked. I would not have known that unless I had seen it modeled by my mother. She had often stated her dismay at how terribly some people were treated in the previous centuries of this country.

As my mother grew older, her health declined. We had lived on a farm in a river valley, and we endured floods as often as yearly. Those floods would fill our basement with water and sometimes the first floor of the house. We were ignorant of the long term effect of mold on the human respiratory system, but we learned the hard way. Allergies plagued our family, and Mom developed severe Asthma and COPD. My father had passed away, so when the time came to get Mom better situated, my brothers and I moved her from the farm to our small town.

In late fall of 2006, I fell on a construction job, and I needed surgery in order to ensure I would continue to be able to walk. My surgery was scheduled, and Mom insisted on coming out to "take care of me." It was rather amusing, because she was far too frail to do a whole lot, but she was wonderful company.

One day an appointment meant I had to be away from home for the morning, and while I was at the doctor's office, my mother called me very upset and nearly hysterical. There were three men in the backyard taking my construction tools. She tried to stop them from stealing, but one of them wrestled her and forced her to the ground triggering a heart attack. She declined rather quickly and passed away about a year later.

As she declined, she reached out to every child and relative and visited each one by phone. She continued to knit, crochet and sew, turning out some of her most amazing artistic quilts in her final years. She shared all she could of her many memories and experiences.

One afternoon she told me that Jesus had stood at the foot of her bed and told her that she had a choice. She could stay with us for a longer time or come home with Him. She wanted to live until she could talk to her youngest daughter one more time, but she didn't ever get to do that. One morning she called me and asked me if it was okay for her to go home. I told her I wanted her to have rest, peace, and total healing from her health issues, and it was okay. She called each of her children and made sure there was peace between her and her children. Then one morning she asked my sister-in-law, Kathy, if she could go home. Kathy told her not to worry and to be where she longed to be. Mom said okay like a child would, laid her head in Kathy's lap, and breathed her last.

None of us have ever wondered whether Mom was in heaven. WE KNOW SHE IS. It is the most peaceful absolute truth I know. A peace that cannot be explained in human words, but Mom is home.

Wm. David Waterman

Wm. David Waterman's life was dramatically changed just two days before Christmas in 1980. On that day, Jesus took his anger, bitterness, and dissatisfaction, and gave him indescribable peace and joy in return. Jesus also healed his addictions to cigarettes and alcohol on December 23, 1980. Today, he lives in New Mexico with his wife, Patti, and also serves as her caregiver.

29

† *A Life Set Free*

▼

by Rena Groot

My story, *A Life Set Free*, was started while sitting under a mosquito net in China. Two years later I finally put all the scribbly notes onto my iPad in a guesthouse in Haifa, Israel. It took several years for God to prepare my heart to write this. I could not have written it sooner. It is written from a place of forgiveness, wholeness, healing, and freedom. Following God has been an incredible adventure. All glory, honor and praise to Him, now and forever. This is a true story about the love and faithfulness of God. This is the story of a life set free.

Jesus Can...

I had a desperately lonely childhood.

I felt abandoned,

rejected, unloved.

Years living

in other people's homes

convinced me

I was the outsider,

not belonging,

so alone.

It sounds crazy,

but I am thankful.

I praise God

because,

He used everything to give me

a greater heart of compassion for others.

Fast forward,

as a twenty-one-year-old university student

I was disillusioned with life

I felt like there was a dark, empty,

hollow space growing inside me.

The emptiness, darkness and hopelessness

of my life overwhelmed me.

I decided I had nothing to live for.

It seemed suicide was better than living.

I contemplated jumping out of a window

on the 18th floor of an apartment building.

While looking at that window,

deliberating about what to do,

I had a vision.

I don't know what else to call it.

It was so strange.

This is hard to explain.

It had been a cloudless day,

but now thick clouds seemed to appear,

just outside the window,

obscuring everything.

I knew they weren't really there,

yet I could see them.

Maybe it was a vision?

I could see through the clouds,

and I saw a throne.

I could not see His face,

but I knew the One seated on that throne

was Jesus.

I knew He was crying for me,

because of the pain,

sadness,

and brokenness of my life.

He spoke,

not with words I could hear,

but with words

that resonated

inside me…

"Rena,

This is not My plan for your life.

If you turn your life over to Me,

I will bring more beauty out of your life

than you could possibly imagine at this moment."

Incredibly,

in a split second,

I saw my entire life.

It was kind of like seeing a high-speed video.

It was too fast to see details,

Yet, I had the impression that it was an amazing,

incredible, beautiful life.

Obviously, I chose to live.

The next part—

the unveiling of the video,

was a process.

I began searching for God.

Everywhere.

I couldn't find Him.

Two years later,

there was an invitation

to a prayer meeting

and I found Him!!!

I was broken-hearted that

My life had grieved Him.

I repented of my sins

and asked Jesus to be my Lord and Savior.

Because of His grace

and mercy,

I was forgiven.

I became a child of God,

adopted into His beautiful, forever family.

No longer alone.

Such amazing love.

If I had died that day,

I would have missed out on so much
God wanted to do in my life and throughout eternity.

This is a story of God's amazing grace.
He saw a sad, lonely girl.
In His great love and compassion,
God pulled me out of darkness
into His amazing light.
He has given me a hope and a future.
The law of the Spirit of life in Christ Jesus
set me free from the law of sin and death!
I found Him.
I am seeking Him still.

Rena Groot

When I was 21-years-old, I went on a quest for God. He took an abandoned, fearful person—someone the world would have considered expendable—and gave me hope and a future. Jesus alone has the power to bring healing to broken lives. Nothing is impossible with God when our lives are surrendered to Him. He can redeem every sorrow. After becoming a Christian, I was able to travel with the Department of Eternal Affairs to Africa, Israel, China, Thailand, Mexico, Haiti, and Greece. I finished university, became a school teacher, married, had four children, and became an artist and a writer. God is able to do more abundantly than we can ask or think. Trust Him. He loves you.

Blog: renagroot.com

30

♡ *Jesus Set Me Free*

<hr>

by Tom Donnan

We are made to be loved. Our deep human desire is to be known and to be loved. What happens when things go horribly wrong? Our human heart, our emotions, are hurt and maybe even damaged. It makes it all the harder for us to be open, to be known, and to be loved. I have heard it said, and know it to be true, that hurt people, hurt people! An offshoot of woundedness is being around or even becoming a toxic person. Deep layers of dysfunction are lived day in and day out. For me, a major issue has been my self-esteem. At the time of this writing, I am sixty-eight years old. Most of my adult life I have lived trying not to remember the first seventeen years. I will talk fondly about the wild and crazy times. They were nothing more than deflection to relieve the inner pain and turmoil of my soul. In my mind, behind the veils of secrecy, festers the puss of hidden pain and memories.

The miracle held within salvation is not an end all. It is a beginning. John 10:10 is a life verse for me: "The thief comes only to steal and kill and destroy; I have come that they may have life, and have it to the full" (NIV). I lived the life that evil had stolen. Rampant sin destroyed my emotional heart and curtailed my mind. Hardened to life, shutting down emotionally, hiding behind a walled fortress, I protected myself from others. Living emotionally vulnerable was not safe until Jesus arrived. I invited Him into my heart and life. I had a dramatic conversion the moment I became born again, meaning that once the Holy Spirit entered my spirit, my life changed for the better. It took time, and I'm not sure exactly when it happened but I became convinced the Lord wanted to heal my inner pain that kept me locked in low self-esteem.

I began to seek out help. I went to many of the self-help groups. One of those groups, ACOA (Adult Children of

Alcoholics) opened my eyes. As others told their life experiences, it came as a shock to me. Their lives sounded a lot like my life's story. Here is where a turn took place. Instead of running from the pain I felt inside, I told the Lord, "Let's do this!" and I ran into it. I made an amazing discovery! God is gentle. He took me into my pain and then we rested. Yes, it was hard, but it happened under His control. Emotions are spiritual in nature. Our loving heavenly Father released provisions to undo what had happened to me in the first seventeen years of my life. This did not happen all at once, but in stages. You see, Jesus had placed it on my heart to pray for healing. This act released Him. He placed my feet upon a spiritual path where the healing began.

Let's do a word picture here. Imagine you are looking at wooden blocks that are two inches square. Each block is numbered from one to hundred so there are ten rows, stacked ten high upon each other. The bottom row is our foundational character elements. Deeply ingrained in us, these hold some of the deepest hurts. But Jesus in his compassion will work on block number nineteen and bring healing before going down to one of the first ten character traits. By healing nineteen, the impact of working on number eight is lightened. For me, number eight was trust. How can you trust any person when those who brought you into this world abused you? Those who are supposed to love and protect you, but don't. What happens when they are the ones from which you need protection?

I'm going to make a jump here to a pivotal discovery. It was in my third year of family reconstruction. This group will take family scenarios and role play them out. It was great information concerning life and what sin does in our lives and families. It brings out the destruction as a result of sin and its consequences. We started with the family of origin or my family, then worked backward to my grandparents and great grandparents. Then the Holy Spirit showed me generational sins. I grew up in a home that had lived this way for generations. Here is the nugget—I was born into a family where there was no way I was going to come out of it OKAY!

As children, we tend to look at ourselves as being the center of the universe. Life revolves around us. I must play a role in why I am being mistreated or abused. NO! This thought process is wrong. It was not about me; it was about sin entering into a family line with no end in sight. No end until Jesus came into my life. Right here is when I discovered that it was not my fault. In the ripple of time, a hundred years before me, the dysfunction raged forward. I let myself off the hook of responsibility. It was not my fault. Even though the response of those older than I told a message, it was something I had done that brought about their dysfunctional actions; it was a lie. A burden dropped off of me. This made it easier to deal with guilt and shame. Block number one for me? I was the reason they abused me. It was I, my character, beliefs, and actions that caused them to act out. Now, in retrospect, in the light and healthiness of my Savior, I see good human behavior. Jesus has been healing me, and He set me free. The ultimate sacrifice? Jesus dying on the cross for my sins brings to me His high esteem. He valued me to the extreme to die for me. This is the foundation of my value and worth that Jesus suffered and died for me.

A Prayer for Generational Sins

I lift up to You, Heavenly Father, Your child receiving this prayer. Please cover them with the blood of Jesus Christ from the top of their heads to the bottom of their feet. Lord, please assign protecting angels, ministering angels, and high-ranking angels to Your child. Father, please forgive their forefathers for the sins they have committed and have caused You pain. We are sorry for the pain it has caused You.

Please forgive them. Lord, please forgive the forefathers who may have known You and forsaken You for other gods. Though they once knew You, they put another god in Your place. We are sorry for the pain their forsaking You has caused. Please forgive them. Heavenly Father, in the name of Jesus, we break off all curses, strongholds, and grounds from their lives, and we cast them off and away from them. In the name of Jesus, they are set free. In Jesus' name. Amen.

Tom Donnan: healingthenation1776@gmail.com

Tom Donnan

Tom Donnan's heart's desire is to share the gospel of Jesus Christ. Life wonderfully changed for him since Jesus came into his life. Now he works to see others blessed by gaining a relationship with Jesus.

Closing Comments

▼

How Jesus Heals Your Hurts and God's Plan of Salvation

Congratulations! You've made it to the end of our second book in the *Jesus Can* Book Series. You've now had the opportunity to read sixty stories of how Jesus came into each writer's life and either healed their hurts or how He saved them through their salvation testimony.

We want to make sure that we have fulfilled our mission to you before you close this book. The mission of this CWC book is to spread the message of how to have an eternal life-saving relationship with Jesus Christ. Our hope is that everyone who reads this book has a personal relationship with Him now. If not, we hope that you start that personal relationship with Jesus by the time you reach the end of these Closing Comments.

On the next few pages are three simple steps for beginning your new life in Christ, just as all thirty of the CWC members/writers featured in this book have done. Receiving your new life in Christ is as simple as ABC...

A—Accept & Admit

Accept the fact that you've done wrong things and admit that you need forgiveness.

> For all have sinned and fall short of the glory of God. Romans 3:23

> For the wages of sin is death. Romans 6:23a

> But if we freely admit our sins when His light uncovers them, He will be faithful to forgive us every time. God is just to forgive us our sins because of

Christ, and He will continue to cleanse us from all unrighteousness. 1 John 1:9

B—Believe & Behave

When you believe that Jesus died on the cross and rose bodily from the grave, paying the penalty for your sins, it changes you. That's because when you change what you believe, it changes how you behave.

For God so loved the world that He gave his one and only Son, that whoever believes in Him shall not perish but have eternal life. For God did not send His Son into the world to condemn the world, but to save the world through Him. John 3:16-17

"The time has come," he said. "The kingdom of God has come near. Repent and believe the good news!" Mark 1:15

They replied, "Believe in the Lord Jesus, and you will be saved—you and your household." Acts 16:31

For what I received I passed on to you as of first importance: that Christ died for our sins according to the Scriptures, that He was buried, that He was raised on the third day according to the Scriptures. 1 Corinthians 15:3-4

C—Confess & Choose

Confess Jesus as your Lord and Savior and choose to follow His plan for your life.

If you declare with your mouth, "Jesus is Lord," and believe in your heart that God raised Him from the dead, you will be saved. For it is with your heart that you believe and are justified, and it is with your mouth that you profess your faith and are saved. Romans 10:9-10

Then Jesus said to his disciples, "Whoever wants to be My disciple must deny themselves and take up their cross and follow Me." Matthew 16:24

For I am not ashamed of the gospel, because it is the power of God that brings salvation to everyone who believes: first to the Jew, then to the Gentile. Romans 1:16

> Everyone who calls on the name of the Lord will be
> saved. Romans 10:13

If you've carefully and prayerfully read through these ABCs, but you still have questions, or you don't feel like anything has changed—no worries. The first "test" of your faith may be to believe that you've been forever changed because the Bible says so, regardless of your feelings.

Another name for the salvation experience is being "born again" (John 3:7). Some people are spiritually born-again with a thirst for God's Word similar to a healthy newborn baby's desire for milk. Other Christian newborns have to cultivate a taste for God's Word. Whether you're spiritually born into that first group, the second, or somewhere in between, it's important to develop the habit of reading God's Word daily. Like that baby needs milk to live, to grow, and to remain healthy, a steady diet of God's Word is essential to the healthy spiritual growth of a newborn Christian, too.

There's a long list of other things that a newborn Christian has in common with a newborn baby. While the innocence of newborns makes them so adorable, it makes them incredibly vulnerable too. The same is true of baby Christians. I'm so grateful to the two older women who counseled me on Sunday, April 10, 1983, the day I asked Jesus to come into my heart and change me. While they rejoiced with me and celebrated the fact that if I had died that very moment, I could rest assured that I'd be on my way to heaven, they also warned me that my decision to trust Jesus had made me an enemy of Satan. My new status as a player on God's team was not to be taken lightly, considering how much the devil hates the fact that he will never be equal to God. These wise women warned me that things in my life could get worse before they got better, now that I was saved. It was only a few weeks before I understood exactly about what they had warned me. Thankfully, even a bad day with Jesus is better than my best day as a sinner destined to join Satan in hell.

The summary of the last few paragraphs, the last few pages, and this entire book series is that Jesus can give you a new life, and when He does, it's just the beginning. Get growing as soon as you're born again. It's one of the few decisions in life that you are assured to never regret.

If you still have some questions about this life-changing decision, I'd suggest visiting NeedHim.org or giving them a call at 888-Need-Him (888-633-3446). You'll be able to connect with a volunteer 24/7 for a live chat or telephone call about "how a relationship with Jesus changes everything."

—Stephanie

P.S. If you have a story to tell, why not share it in an upcoming book of our series? It's easy to apply to become a member of the Christian Writers Collective—the authors of each *Jesus Can* book. Just submit your well-written, 500-750 word testimony using the CONTACT US form on our website, www.christianwriterscollective.com. If selected, your testimony will appear in the next book in the series.

www.ingramcontent.com/pod-product-compliance
Lightning Source LLC
Chambersburg PA
CBHW051521150726
47997CB00001B/331